Jesus' Words for Teens

STANDING TALL

Leader's Guide

Taken from the books of

Matthew, Mark, Luke, and John

along with other relevant Bible references

Candice Mary Thomas

Published by DTJ Press

Copyright © 2021 Candice Mary Thomas

All images designed either by Freepik, www.Freepik.com or www.Pixabay.com.

No part of this book may be reproduced or transmitted in any form or by an means, electronic or mechanical, including photocopying and recording, or by any information storage or retrieval system, except as may be expressly permitted in writing by the author. Requests for permission should be emailed to dtjpress@gmail.com.

The *Jesus' Words for Teens: Standing Tall* study is the second in the series of text courses for teens in the area of Biblical Studies.

ISBN 978-1-7332133-7-0

Scripture quotations, other than noted, are taken from the Holy Bible, New Living Translation, copyright © 1996, 2004, 2015 by Tyndale House Foundation. Used by permission of Tyndale House Publishers, Inc., Carol Stream, Illinois 60188. All rights reserved.

Printed in the United States of America.

Dedicated to my loving husband, Terry,

without whom I may never have accepted

Jesus Christ as my personal Lord and Savior.

Because He lives and has redeemed me,

I have a new song to sing.

Psalm 40:1-3

In Memory of

Pastor Vaughan Nelson

who was instrumental in my journey to

knowing, loving, and accepting

Jesus Christ

as my personal Savior!

To God be all honor, praise, and glory

...now and forevermore!

TABLE OF CONTENTS

Letter to Leaders i
Definintions/Format ii
Introduction 9
Digging In--Week One--Group Time--*Standing Tall* 10
    Personal Time Day One 23
    Personal Time Day Two 26
    Personal Time Day Three 37
    Personal Time Day Four 41
Digging In--Week Two--Group Time--*Man's Laws over God's???* 48
    Personal Time Day One 59
    Personal Time Day Two 65
    Personal Time Day Three 68
    Personal Time Day Four 69
Digging In--Week Three--Group Time--*Blind Leading the Blind* 70
    Personal Time Day One 80
    Personal Time Day Two 83
    Personal Time Day Three 85
    Personal Time Day Four 89
Digging In--Week Four--Group Time--*Marriage Part One* 93
    Personal Time Day One 103
    Personal Time Day Two 109
    Personal Time Day Three 111
    Personal Time Day Four 114
Digging In--Week Five--Group Time--*Marriage Part Two* 117
    Personal Time Day One 138
    Personal Time Day Two 148
    Personal Time Day Three 149
    Personal Time Day Four 151

Digging In--Week Six--Group Time--*Divorce* 152
    Personal Time Day One 168
    Personal Time Day Two 173
    Personal Time Day Three 177
    Personal Time Day Four 179
Digging In--Week Seven--Group Time--*Persecution* 185
    Personal Time Day One 194
    Personal Time Day Two 195
    Personal Time Day Three 197
    Personal Time Day Four 198
Digging In--Week Eight--*Personal Reflection*... 199
Acknowledgments 211
Notes/Sources 213
Apprendix A--***Prayer for Salvation*** 217
Glossary 219
Bibliography 220
Notes 221

Dear Leaders,

Thank you for your willingness to serve God by mentoring our youth, leading them into a greater understanding of Scripture, God's plan for salvation, and His will for their lives. I feel it is of utmost importance for our children and youth to become firmly rooted in the knowledge of God's Word and in a growing love relationship with Him. When God put it into my heart to write a study based on Jesus' words, it was with the urging that these generations might see His return. Who knows? But when God calls, a believer follows. And, as the parable of the ten virgins with lamps teaches, it is always best to be prepared.

As I write from the viewpoint of one in her seventies, I readily admit that I grew up in a much more innocent age. Cigarettes and drinking might have been high school issues, but certainly not the prevalence of drugs, anxiety, depression, splintered families, gender identity issues, and the political anger and unrest we see today. Therefore, I would ask you to expand on my ideas, giving current day examples from your lives and those of others, making questions and examples relevant to today's youth. Also, you will note that I have kept my answers brief, so please feel free to add complete details.

Guiding youth into a greater knowledge of God's Word is the path that leads to wisdom—wisdom that builds strong roots and a heart relationship with God that says, "I believe You. I trust You. I will fear no evil, *'for what can man do unto me?'* " **[Heb. 13:6]** So as our world grows more and more like that of Noah's times, we have peace because of our one great hope: the Name of our Lord and Savior.

Jesus Christ.

May each of you be blessed with a double dose of wisdom and discernment as you journey forth, teaching God's Holy Word.

Candice Thomas

DEFINITIONS

General Study: Digging into God's Word, generating, and writing down answers

Person Time Discussion: Discussion of the previous week's Personal Time Answers

Prayer Time: Praying for each other, our families, local and national governments, needs of those in other countries, ourselves, etc.

Leader's Desire: Campfire, games, visiting, more snacks, closing worship song, etc.

POSSIBLE 90-MINUTE SMALL GROUP FORMAT
8 Week Study

Opening prayer
Worship Time:	10 minutes
General Study:	20 minutes
Snack Break:	5 minutes
Personal Time Discussion:	25 minutes
Leader's Desire:	30 minutes

15 WEEK STUDY (RECOMMENDED)

Alternate *General Study* one week with *Personal Time* the next *Discussion* the following week. Extend *Study/Discussion* time, *Snack Break*, and *Leader's Desire*. This allows for more in-depth discussion.

FAMILY STUDY

Parents: Work through the *Group Study* together. Follow up with *Personal Time Discussion*, being sensitive to areas that your teens may find hard to share with you. This may prompt an opportunity for all family members to be open with each other.

(Note: Unless otherwise noted, this study uses the New Living Translation [NLT], which is easy to read and understand. Today's youth should find it relevant and relational.)

INTRODUCTION

"I pray that from His (God's) glorious, unlimited resources He will empower you with inner strength through His Spirit. Then Christ will make His home in your hearts as you trust in Him. ***Your roots will grow down into God's love and keep you strong."*** **[Eph. 3:16-17]**

Your preteen and teen years can be some of the most exciting years of your life. They may also bring on growing pains—unfamiliar emotions and questions about who you are, what lies in your future, and concern over the crazy world we live in. You may question, "How am I to live during these times?"

Here is the good news. Just as you have a manual to teach you how to drive well, there is another manual to guide you in how to live your life well, and that is the Bible. By studying God's Word, you will grow to understand how very, very much He loves you—so much, in fact, that He sacrificed His only Son to give you eternal life, if you so choose. You will come to understand that He wants to have not a distant, but a personal, loving relationship with you.

In **Isaiah 55:11**, God reveals a truth of Scripture : *"…so shall my Word be that goes out from my mouth; it shall not return to me empty, but it shall accomplish that which I purpose, and shall succeed in the thing for which I sent it."* ESV What does this mean? As you study Scripture, His Word will lead you and teach you; your heart will soften and change as you learn about God's great love, compassion, mercy, and steadfastness. Your trust in Him will grow, and with a heart devoted to Him, you will be able to live **standing tall**.

This is my prayer for you: As you study God's Word, may our faithful and loving Father bless you with the knowledge, wisdom, and strength you will need to **stand tall** for truth, and with changed hearts filled with love and devotion to Him, glorify Him in all you do.

Candice Mary Thomas

DIGGING IN – WEEK ONE – GROUP TIME

God is love. He does not have love; He is love itself! By this, I don't refer to romantic love or a love based on meeting any conditions. God's love is so great, so all-encompassing, it is without conditions. This is **agape love**—a love far above anything we can imagine! What we do know about this extraordinary love, however, is that God *poured it out* according to His purpose as He created the universe, our earth, all life, and our ultimate salvation through Christ Jesus.

Let's look back in time. *After six days of creative effort, "God looked over all He had made, and He saw that it was very good!"* **[Gen. 1:31]** The earth was perfect; all was pure, designed for life in abundance.

Man was naked, but knew no shame. **(Gen. 2:25)** Then came Satan, cast from heaven because of his rebellion and betrayal of God: *"How you are fallen from heaven, O shining star, son of the morning! You have been thrown down to the earth, you who destroyed the nations of the world. For you said to yourself, 'I will ascend to heaven and set my throne above God's stars. I will preside on the mountain of the gods far away in*

the north. I will climb to the highest heaven and be like the Most High.' "
[Isaiah 14:12-14]

With a third of the angels at his side, Satan became a roaring lion, raging against God with one desire—to destroy anything and anyone who stood for the Creator of all.

Thus began the war between good and evil—good being God and His way…evil being Satan and his. While God desires *life* in every form, Satan desires *death* in every form. He is a deceiver, liar, thief, and murderer. Through deception and lies, *"Satan, who is the god of this world, has blinded the minds of those who don't believe."* **[2 Cor. 4:4a]** Thus, Peter warns us, *"Stay alert! Watch out for your great enemy, the devil. He prowls around like a roaring lion, looking for someone to devour."* **[1 Peter 5:8]**

Look up **John 10:10** and **Luke 22:31**. What do these verses tell you? **John 10:10** Satan's purpose is to steal, kill, and destroy; Jesus' purpose is to give a rich and satisfying life. **Luke 22:31** Satan asks God to sift each of us as wheat. This means that all of us are in a struggle against evil.

What does this mean for us? Perhaps you have heard the

term, **stand tall**. This is very different from *standing up straight* or *straightening up*, terms you may be familiar with! Is there a difference between those two? You better believe it! One concerns posture (yes, it really is better for your overall health!), and one concerns attitude (so really, were you rolling your eyes?!). But **standing tall**…what on earth does that mean? Take a guess and write your definition here:

_____
_____
_____
_____
_____
_____

Standing tall is extremely important for people of all ages and has been throughout all time. This idiomatic phrase *stands* for behavior that is brave and unyielding when knowing one is in the right; it means there will be no retreat from confrontation, danger, or adversity.1 When your heart grows in love for the Lord, your trust will also, enabling you to **stand tall**. You will develop convictions and *unshakable unbreakables* that lead you over life's hurdles and ordinary trials as well as the temptations and situations Satan will design to draw you away from God. What are *unshakable unbreakables*? Based on convictions, they are commitments you make now that will help you follow God's will when you face tough choices and decisions in life.

So how old do you need to be to have a love strong enough, a heart devoted enough, and a trust great enough in God upon which you can develop convictions and *unshakable unbreakables*? Ten? Twenty? Thirty, like Jesus? Let's take a moment and answer these questions before we look at Jesus' words and His steadfast example of **standing tall**.

Enter Daniel, Hananiah, Mishael, and Azariah, the last three better known as Shadrach, Meshach, and Abednego. **(Daniel 1:6)**

Most theologians agree these boys were somewhere between the ages of twelve and fourteen when they were captured and dragged from Jerusalem to Babylon by King Nebuchadnezzar.2 WOW! Maybe about your age…not very old! Let's find out more about these youth.

"Then the king commanded Ashpenaz, his chief eunuch, to bring some of the people of Israel, both of the royal family and of the nobility, youths without blemish, of good appearance and skillful in all wisdom, endowed with knowledge, understanding learning, and competent to stand in the king's palace, and to teach them the literature and language of the Chaldeans." **[Daniel 1:4] ESV**

"Then the king ordered Ashpenaz, his chief of staff, to bring to the palace some of the young men of Judah's royal family and other noble families, who had been brought to Babylon as captives. "Select only strong,

healthy, and good-looking young men," he said. *"Make sure they are well versed in every branch of learning, are gifted with knowledge and good judgment, and are suited to serve in the royal palace. Train these young men in the language and literature of Babylon."* **[Daniel 1:4] NLT**

1. What class of families did Daniel, Hananiah, Mishael, and Azariah come from? They were from royal or noble families.

_____
_____

2. Describe their physical characteristics. Each was without blemish, strong, healthy, and handsome. **(Daniel 1:4)**

3. Do you know of any young men or women who are rich, strong, healthy, and handsome or beautiful? (Perhaps this describes you!)   Yes____   No____

If *yes*, describe their personalities, e.g. are they humble or arrogant? Are they obedient to authority, or do they demand their own way? Are they selfless, being a servant, or selfish, wanting to be served? Are they pampered, or do they have a strong work ethic? What would you say about their hearts? What is their focus in life?   In terms of these questions, how would you describe yourself?

_____
_____
_____
_____

Consider these things as we continue studying the attitudes and behaviors of Daniel, Hananiah, Mishael, and Azariah.

4. In Babylon, what kind of training did the four youth receive and for how long were they to be trained? They were to be trained for three years, studying every aspect of Babylonian culture and all branches of learning, such as the Babylonian language, literature, and science (which would include astrology).

5. According to **Daniel 1:4**, what was the purpose of this training? The youth were to become suitable *to serve in the royal palace.*

The NLT version of Daniel 1:4 makes it sound as if Hananiah, Mishael, and Azariah would immediately be placed in the king's service after training. The ESV version makes this a little more clear, as it is most probable that the four were being trained as satraps—provincial governors—who would be placed in charge of the provinces where Jewish captives lived. The Babylonian plan was that, as former royalty, the four would be respected, listened to, and peace would be kept. Satraps occasionally met in the king's court to represent their provinces, so the four youth would be *"serving in the royal palace."*

6. Read **Daniel 1:6-7**. What happened in these verses, and why do you think Ashpenaz, the chief of Nebuchadnezzar's staff, did this? In order to be *suitable* to serve as a satrap for the Babylonians, all of the youths' Israelite heritage had to be removed and their faith in the One true God replaced with that of false gods. For this reason, Ashpenaz gave each youth a name associated with a Babylonian god.

Explain to the teens the changes and the meanings of each name:

Daniel = "God is my judge" to Belteshezzar = "Bel will protect."[3] Bel was the common name for Babylon's city and national god, Marduk. Originally associated with thunder, he later became known as the lord of the heavens and earth and creator of all.[4]

Hananiah = "God has been gracious" to Shadrach = "the command of Aku"[5] Aku was the moon god.[6]

Mishael – "Who is what God is?" to Meshach = "Belonging to Aku"[7]

Azariah = "The Lord has helped" to Abednego [8] = "Servant of Nebo" Nebo was the Babylonian god of wisdom.[9]

Read **Daniel 1:8-15**.

7. How was the faith of the four youth tested? They were commanded by the king to eat his food and wine.

To eat or not to eat . . .
That is the question!

Daniel was determined not to defile himself by eating food God deemed unacceptable, so he asked that he and his three friends be fed vegetables and water.

8. How did God reward their faith and steadfastness to His commands? They looked better nourished and healthier than any of the other youth.

In spite of their birth heritage, Daniel, Shadrach, Meshach, and Abednego were not prideful, haughty, nor disdainful. Rather, they took the gifts God had given them, *"an unusual aptitude for understanding every aspect of literature and wisdom,"* and to Daniel, *"the special ability to interpret the meanings of visions and dreams"* **[Daniel 1:17]**, and without abandoning their faith, worked hard, using these gifts to learn what was asked of them. Any thoughts of their noble standings or future in Israel were long gone. The fact that, in most likelihood, the four were made eunuchs contributed to this. While the book of Daniel does not state they were eunuchs, when we go to the book of Isaiah, we read: *" 'The time is coming when everything in your palace—all the treasures stored up by your ancestors until now—will be carried off to Babylon. Nothing will be left,' says the LORD. 'Some of your very own sons will be taken away into exile. They will become eunuchs who will serve in the palace of Babylon's king.' "* **[Isaiah 39: 6-7]** Being eunuchs, captives who became leaders in Babylon, such as Daniel, Shadrach, Meshach, and Abednego, would not have children who might later fight to take over the kingdom.

We know the four had aptitude. How do we know they worked hard? Read **Daniel 1:18-20** to learn the answer.

9. After talking with the youth, what was the king's response? He was more impressed with Daniel, Shadrach, Meshach, and Abednego than any other youth. He also found them ten times more capable than any of his magicians and enchanters when he desired wisdom and "balanced" judgment in matters. **(Daniel 1:20)** In fact, he was so impressed with them that rather than placing them as satraps in charge of Israelite captives, he placed them in positions above the Babylonians! Of course, this was a recipe for jealousy and problems with Babylonian leaders!

10. What does the king's response teach us? There is an enormous gulf between aptitude, knowledge, and wisdom. Aptitude, or the natural ability to do or learn things quickly, if not applied is

worthless. It is the study, the drill, the stretching through challenge, and the application of those things that bring knowledge and wisdom. The fact that the king found Daniel, Shadrach, Meshach, and Abednego ten times more wise and balanced in their judgment than others demonstrates that they worked hard, and when they were placed in positions of responsibility, their work paid off.

APTITUDE . . .

STUDY . . .

KNOWLEDGE . . .

DRILL . . .

WISDOM . . .

So far we've learned that Daniel, Shadrach, Meshach, and Abednego worked hard to learn what the Babylonians asked of them, accepted their circumstances, and yet somehow remained dedicated to the one true God. How do you think this was possible?

I like to believe that Daniel, Shadrach, Meshach, and Abednego had deeply committed parents who loved God wholeheartedly and followed His command to teach their children well, in spite of the fact that many in their nation were rebelling so much against God that He would allow the Babylonians to discipline them by taking them into captivity when their children were in their early teens. *"They did not remain faithful to my covenant, so I turned my back on them, says the Lord."* **[Hebrews 8:9b]** These parents most likely took to heart, *"Hear, O Israel: The Lord our God, the Lord is one! You shall love the Lord your God with all your heart, with all your soul, and with all your strength. And these words which I command you today shall be in your heart. You shall teach them diligently to your children, and shall talk of them when you sit in your house, when you walk by the way, when you lie down, and when you rise up."* **[Deut. 6:4-7]**

So I believe these parents daily obeyed God by teaching their children to love God in the same way they had been instructed—with all their hearts, souls, and strength. I also believe that obedience to God's commandments became a way of life for Daniel, Shadrach, Meshach, and Abednego. Their actions in Babylon prove how they fully respected God's first commandment: *"I am the LORD your God, who rescued you from the land of Egypt, the place of your slavery. You must not have any other god but Me. You must not make for yourself an idol of any kind or an image of anything in the heavens or on the earth or in the sea. You must not bow down to them or worship them, for I, the LORD your God, am a jealous God who will not tolerate your affection for any other gods."* **[Exodus 20:2-4a]**

God's laws, then, were not just something Daniel, Shadrach, Meshach, and Abednego obeyed; they became the heart, drive and mission of these young men. Their obedience to these commandments demonstrated hearts fully committed to God, and in acting as they did in Babylon, the four honored Him by displaying complete trust in His power, promises, and protection—proved to them by the mighty miracles God provided in leading their nation from slavery in Egypt to freedom in the Promised Land.

God parted the Red Sea and provided manna in the Sinai Desert.

Sinai Desert

11. Using the above information, describe how Daniel, Shadrach, Meshach, and Abednego resisted temptation in Babylon and **stood tall** when threatened with death. They knew exactly what they believed and why they believed as they did. They were students of Scripture and had memorized much of it. They were convinced that God was the one true God who loved them and deserved their complete love and devotion in return, and they knew He was to be trusted and obeyed at all times and at all cost.

12. Give at least one example of a conviction you believe Daniel, Shadrach, Meshach, and Abednego had and an **unshakable unbreakable** based on this. Example: **Conviction**—Although my name is changed, I know my true identity; I am created by the one true God in His image. *Unshakable Unbreakable*—No person or circumstance will convince me that I am not who God made me to be, and I will live accordingly.

_____
_____
_____
_____
_____

Read **Daniel 3** and **Daniel 6**. Discuss the convictions and *unshakable unbreakables* Daniel, Shadrach, Meshach, and Abednego had in these instances. Open a discussion with the teens. Talk about what *complete trust* is.

Now, let's review a question initially asked: How old do you have to be to have convictions and *unshakable unbreakables* in order to **stand tall**? Again, lead the student discussion, e.g. there is no age requirement, but it does take diligence and self-discipline to study God's Word, burying the truths of Scripture deep within our spirits. It requires praying and becoming completely devoted to God, placing Him foremost in our lives, allowing Him to change our hearts from selfishness to selflessness, becoming deeply devoted to Him, loving Him with our *all,* and loving others. All this requires complete trust in our Almighty God, especially when facing the most dire circumstances…"*Even when I walk through the darkest valley, I will not be afraid, for you are close beside me. Your rod and your staff protect and comfort me.*" **[Psalm 23:4]**

Topics, therefore, that you may wish to discuss include studying the Bible, memorizing Scripture, helping teens develop a firm understanding of their Christian beliefs and being able to defend those, prayer, confession of sin, the daily seeking of being filled with the Holy Spirit, and seeking changes in their lives that demonstrate hearts totally devoted to God.

Week One – Day One – Personal Time

1. Over the years, if you've attended church or youth group, you have heard and been taught *truths* about God. Write down as many of these as possible, each on a separate line. _____

_____
_____
_____
_____
_____
_____
_____
_____
_____
_____
_____
_____
_____
_____
_____
_____
_____
_____
_____
_____
_____
_____
_____

2. Go back over your list. Do you know if the things you've written are truths, or could any of them be false, being based upon current popular beliefs and theology? Place a T above the statements you believe are true and a question mark above statements about which you are not certain. These should be discussed with your group later.

After any questions you have, jot a note. Example: God exists. If you've written a question mark, write, *"Does He really?"* Here are other possible statements and questions you might have: "God is good." *Is He really?* "I should obey all God's commands." *Do all of His commandments still apply today?* "God desires life and goodness for me." *How can I believe this when so many bad things have happened in my life?* "There is only one true God, the God of Abraham, Isaac, and Jacob." *Don't all religions pray to the same God and all roads lead to heaven?* "Jesus is the only path to eternal life with God." *Don't all good people go to heaven?*

WHAT IS TRUTH ? ? ?

You may feel that you are making yourself vulnerable by making your questions known, but answers to these questions are critical! If in the end you feel you can't be open with your concerns, schedule a time with your group leader to discuss these things. Be sure to answer all teen questions thoroughly during Personal Discussion time, as they will be critical in the teens' walk with Christ.

4. Are there any truths in which you firmly believe? If so, based upon these, write down at least one conviction and

unshakable unbreakable you can cling to throughout your life, no matter the circumstance.

Week One – Day Two – Personal Time

Daniel, Shadrach, Meshach, and Abednego were apparently raised by devout Israelite parents who were instructed by God not only to teach their children His commandments, but to pass on their heritage as God's chosen people and nation. In doing so, children learned how cherished they were by God. Even though they were sinners, He showered His love on them through mighty and powerful miracles, protecting them and providing for their every need.

We might think that it was the result of being taught all these things and studying the Scriptures that Daniel, Shadrach, Meshach, and Abednego exemplified living in obedience to God. But there was much more involved than this! Obedience demands not just head knowledge; it demands a faithful, loving, and trusting heart! As the four learned of God, His love, provision, and care, their hearts were changed from being focused on self to being focused on the One they loved. It was this love that caused them to honor God in all they did, even to the point of death.

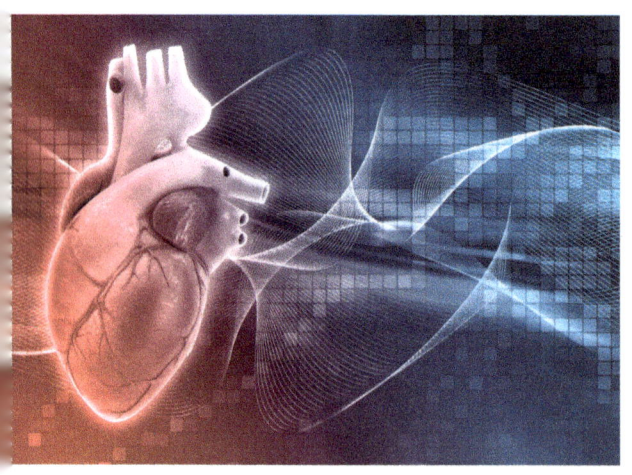

You possibly have been raised by devout Christian parents who, having accepted Jesus as their personal Savior, are raising you in their faith. This is just what God wants! However, as your parents' child, you are an individual with *choices* to make. You can't love God and accept Jesus as your Savior just because your parents have done so.

Then there's the possibility you may have been raised in a non-Christian family whose life actions are totally opposed to loving God and/or accepting Jesus as Savior. You ***still have choices*** to make...***choices*** that affect your eternity.

Pray for a time, and then ask yourself these questions:

1. Why do I attend church and/or youth group? Is it because my parents make me, I want to be with my friends, or am I lonely? Or, is it because I love God and desire to be changed more and more into the image of Christ? _____

_____
_____
_____
_____
_____
_____
_____
_____

2. Have I truly accepted Jesus as my personal Savior? If not, what is keeping me from doing so? _____

_____

3. What is my faith or lack of faith based upon? _____

4. How can I grow in my trust of God and His promises? Ideas: Study Scripture, learning God's nature—how He is a trustworthy promise keeper who, being omniscient, knows what is best for each of us, even when we pass through life's toughest trials. Pray and watch how God answers your prayers according to His perfect will…which may not be ours..but lead to the outcomes He desires. Read testimonies of those who have come to accept Jesus as Savior, especially those who were once atheists.

5. Can I say that I *"love the Lord my God with all my heart, mind, spirit, and strength?"* **[Mark 12:30]** _____

Explain by giving examples. Then, whether your answer is *yes* or *no*, describe how the above verse can become your heart and life. _____
_____
_____
_____
_____
_____

Candice's Story: I was by nature an introvert, and as a teenager, was extremely shy and uncertain of myself. It didn't help that I was raised by an extremely domineering mother who didn't allow any opinion but her own to prevail and who often resorted to verbal abuse to control my brother and me. (Later, as an adult, I worked through the heart issues I had with my mom and do love her.) My brother, who was four years older, unfortunately rebelled. When caught, he was punished by being spanked with a wire coat hanger. I didn't have to think twice about not wanting that to

happen to me, so I responded to conflict by giving in to whatever my mother wanted. This learned behavior led to my becoming a people pleaser in order to feel accepted by her, my peers, and others. So when push came to shove, I would give in.

You may think I should have been stronger—that I had my faith to fall back on. But the truth is, I had never placed my faith in Jesus—in fact, I had no idea of what that meant! For sure, I was taught the Lord's Prayer, was sent to church on Sundays, but my family did not attend church, talk about God, or read the Bible. (My brother would walk me to church, take off, then return to walk me home. My parents never found out because I never ratted on him; I couldn't stand to see him get punished with that wire coat hanger!)

The church I attended was legalistic, and I was taught that disobeying church rules would lead me straight into the **vast, yawning hole** of hell. Fearing this, I tried my best not to sin but had to rely on my own standards, and, as I just wrote, I was used to "giving in" to the pressure of others. Without the Holy Spirit living within me and guiding me, righteous living was impossible…not a great way to live!

Once I accepted Christ as my Savior, however, my heart became softened, and I began to change. As I studied Scripture, I learned I was truly a beloved child of God—that He loved me so much He sent His Son to suffer the penalty of my sins and enable me to inherit eternal life with Him. I learned that it was **not** following rules that earned salvation, but Jesus' selfless sacrifice on the cross; that it was **not** following rules that cultivated righteous living, but a heart set on loving, living for, and serving God.

I came to know God's love for me was all-encompassing and that I could trust Him at all times, no matter "how hot the furnace." I felt a fire in my heart, desiring all children and youth to know what I had missed in being raised as I had been without Christ, which led to years of sin. How clear it was that I would have lived life differently had I known Christ as my Savior as a child!

I have no words to let you know how forever grateful I will be to God that at the age of thirty-two, He used my husband to lead me to Jesus. With my heart changed and full trust placed in the Lord, I began to **stand tall** in my journey to let others know what Christ has done for me. I began teaching Sunday school, leading children's church and later high school and college age Bible studies; I became a Christian school teacher and administrator, and now I write this study, attempting to relate to you some of what God has taught me through my forty-one years of walking with Jesus and the joy He has brought into my life through loving His Son.

My fervent prayer is that God's Word may place such a thirst in your spirits that it won't be quenched until you fully submit to Jesus, loving Him with all your hearts, minds, spirits, and strength, serving Him with whatever spiritual gifts and natural talents He has given you. May your lives shine as a witness to others as you live in love and obedience to our Almighty God!

Terry's Story: Our family, like many, went to church on Easter, Christmas, and sometimes on Mother's Day. My dad was a

Los Angeles policeman who worked rotating shifts, and I don't recall him attending any services until I was in a Christmas play in the fifth grade.

We moved to Oregon in 1959, and when my grandparents retired in 1962, they moved onto our property in Tenmile, Oregon, as it had two houses on eighty acres of land, pastures, and lots of trees—lots and lots of trees!

Grandma Zelma was a Bible reading, church going, praying woman. She found a small church with a congregation of about

twenty-five people a few miles from our houses and started attending regularly. I decided I wanted to go to church with Grandma, but if I wanted to go with her, I had to be in her car at 8:45 a.m. on Sunday or she was gone. I remember several times running down our driveway to cut Grandma off before she hit the road and headed to church!

I was the only one from my family who went to church with Grandma; not even Grandpa Glen went, but that didn't stop Grandma Zelma! Sunday morning, Sunday night, Wednesday… she was there, and I often went to the weekly meetings with her if it didn't interfere with any of the sports I was involved in at the time.

With the church being so small, it turned out that Grandma was my Sunday school teacher, and with her leading, I accepted Jesus as my Savior in the seventh grade. I was baptized in Olalla Creek a few miles away from the church. Glad it was in the summer!

All through middle and high school I attended this small Tenmile Assembly of God Church with Grandma. It was led by Pastor Jim Black, who was a timber faller during the weekdays. His wife played the piano, his son played the accordion, and his daughter played the violin. That was our musical arrangement, and in the words of some, it was "precious." All the old hymns were played, and to show you the need of volunteers, I often led the singing from stage. I hit all the notes, often in the same verse…"precious"!)

The beginning of some of my later years of *wandering* began when, even though I had confessed my belief in Christ and had been baptized, I was taught that in order to be a *complete Christian,* I had to speak in tongues. Believe me, I tried! In a small side room, I spent hours praying and praying for this, but nothing happened! I therefore doubted that I was truly a Christian.

During the summer between my junior and senior years of high school, a tragic accident occurred that, along with feeling I was not a *complete Christian,* changed the course of my life for many years. Pastor Jim had hired his son, James, to trim limbs for him as he logged, and one day when felling a tree, its heavy branches hit James, killing him on the spot.

This tragedy took Pastor Jim out of the pulpit, out of the church, and sadly out of his family. He moved away and within a short period of time, committed suicide. I thought, "If a great man of God could do this, what hope is there for me to handle crises, troubles, and the pressures of life?" Besides, I wasn't really a Christian, was I? I started to drift. I hadn't been taught the truth… that we don't become Christian by doing any works, including speaking in tongues, but we are saved by placing our faith in Jesus Christ alone. This is God's grace! *"God saved you by His grace when you believed. And you can't take credit for this; it is a gift from God."* **[Eph. 2:8]**

I drifted for years, and even though I didn't recognize it, God always had his hand upon me, letting me walk away from a car crash that should have killed me, saving me several times when I had parachute malfunctions while in Air Force Para-Rescue, and other situations in which only God could have delivered me from harm.

It wasn't until I was thirty years old, that God led me to a non-denominational service where I recommitted my life to the Lord. Since that time, it's been a journey of growth in the Lord, learning the true meaning of God's gift of grace and walking as Christ would have me. I've had the wonderful privilege of leading my wife to Christ and bringing up my family in the faith, and I believe I owe all this to the faithful prayers and example of Grandma Zelma.

Your Story: Write about how you are being raised. Are your parents *born again believers?* Do they talk to you about God the Father, Jesus, and the Holy Spirit? Do they encourage you to read and study your Bible to become wise? Do they pray and show this by example? Do they encourage you to obey God's commandments, explaining why you should? Do they exemplify loving the Lord God with all their hearts, spirits, minds, and strength, teaching you how this has changed them and how important it is for you to love God with your *all?*

Write about all of this and the positives and negatives you see in the development of your faith and beliefs. (Please pray and really think about your answers before you write. This should take some serious contemplation.)

Week One – Day Three – Personal Time

Choose one of the following:

    1. Have you ever been encouraged to do something in direct opposition to your faith? Write what you were asked or encouraged to do. Who was the person or persons urging you to do this, and what was their reasoning behind this? What was your response? Why do you feel you responded this way? If you responded in an ungodly manner, do you ever wish you had responded differently? If you responded the way God would wish, what helped you to do so?

_____
_____
_____
_____
_____
_____
_____
_____
_____
_____
_____
_____
_____

C H O I C E S

OR

2. Is there anything in your life you regret doing or not doing? Was there sin associated with this? Would a heart dedicated to God with convictions and *unshakable unbreakables* have helped you to make a different choice or decision? Why or why not? _____

_____
_____
_____
_____
_____
_____
_____
_____
_____
_____
_____
_____
_____
_____
_____
_____
_____

C H O I C E S

After responding to either number one or two above, talk to God. He is your greatest champion, always on your side, always ready to defend you and heal old wounds. *"But he was pierced for our rebellion, crushed for our sins. He was beaten so we could be whole. He was whipped so we could be healed."* **[Isaiah 53:5]**

Be open with God! If a decision you made in the past brings pain and bad memories of what happened, give it to Jesus. *"Come to me, all of you who are weary and carry heavy burdens, and I will give you rest. Take My yoke upon you. Let me teach you, because I am humble and gentle at heart, and you will find rest for your souls. For My yoke is easy to bear, and the burden I give you is light."* **[Matthew 11:28-30]**

Always remember that if you are a believer in Jesus, you are ***never*** to feel guilt, shame, or condemnation. **(Romans 8:1)** So when Satan's soldiers (demons) attack you with reminders of the past, shout ***NO***! Remind yourself that your heavenly Father loves you more than you can imagine! He is always willing to forgive your sins if you simply admit them, confess, and ask His forgiveness. *"But if we confess our sins to Him, He is faithful and just to forgive us our sins and to cleanse us from all wickedness."* **[1 John 1:9]** Using one hand, point to the palm of the other to remind yourself that Jesus took all sin upon Himself at the cross and paid for those in full. Your debt and my debt have been canceled. Repeat as many times as you need: ***My debt has been canceled!***

*He *paid* for my sins,*
your sins,
all sins

in full!

Jesus paid once for all!
1 Peter 3:18

Week One – Day Four – Personal Time

"All slaves should show full respect for their masters so they will not bring shame on the name of God and His teaching." **[1 Tim 6:1]**

Although Daniel, Shadrach, Meshach, and Abednego did not have the advantage of the teachings of the New Testament, they definitely exemplified the above verse. Because of their love of God, they never shamed Him, taking a rebellious or easy road once in captivity. So in spite of being made slaves; in spite of being strong, handsome, smart, and of noble heritage; in spite of eating differently than others in the king's court; and in spite of having to study hard to prove themselves acceptable to the king, each accepted his destiny and used his God-given abilities to respect his new masters, thus honoring the one true God in every way.

Think about it: If you were in the place of these young men, how would you have reacted when tested? Use your answers to the following to help you know.

1. Have you studied Scripture enough to understand God's commandments and to have a heart totally devoted to Him so that you know how He wants you to live? If not, what would it take to change this, and is learning about God, studying His commandments, and developing a loving relationship with Him something you desire to do? _____

_____

_____

_____

_____
_____
_____
_____
_____

If so, it is time for you to write down a conviction and an *unshakable unbreakable* that will be your call to **stand tall**. In either case, write your answers below.

_____
_____
_____
_____
_____
_____
_____

2. Are you "sold out" on God? Is your heart totally devoted to Him and your faith strong enough to trust and obey Him at all times, even if doing so leads to losing friends, family, or ultimately your life? Times are changing, and we don't know, but it could be that one day you will be faced with either meeting governmental demands in direct opposition to God's laws or losing your life. Are you prepared for this? Explain. _____

_____

_____

_____

_____

_____

_____

_____

_____

3. Are any of us strong enough to face similar situations to those of Daniel, Shadrach, Meshach, and Abednego? Perhaps, but for most, the answer would be "no." Discuss how scared the apostles were when Jesus was tried and crucified, before they received the Holy Spirit. Examples: Peter's denial of Jesus **(Matthew 18:25-27; Luke 22:54-62)**; the disciples fleeing from Christ in the Garden of Gethsemane **(Mark 14:50)**; **Matthew 26:56)**; the disciples hiding behind locked doors **(John 20:19).**

Today's Garden of

Gethsemane

Jesus' disciples were not like the four Israelite youth. When Christ was arrested in the Garden of Gethsemane, they feared for their lives and fled.

Olive trees in the Garden of Gethsame.

Unlike Daniel, Shadrach, Meshach, and Abednego, who had to rely on their own knowledge of God's love, His power and wrath, we have a Helper available to give us the strength needed to **stand tall** before others in obedience to God. Read **John 14:15-17** and **Acts 1:8** to discover who that Helper is.

4. Who is that Helper? The Holy Spirit.

5. Give some examples of the Holy Spirit as helper. Have the teens turn to the book of Acts, and read passages where the Holy Spirit transformed Jesus' disciples, enabling them to conquer their fears, **stand tall** against the crowds, and spread Jesus' gospel. Examples: Peter, who denied Christ three times, now fearlessly preaches to the crowds about Jesus and salvation **(Acts 2:14-40)**; Peter and John are arrested, taken before the council of rulers, elders, and teachers of religious law, then boldly testify about Christ. **(Acts 4: 1-21)**

6. How does the Holy Spirit come to live in us? The moment we ask Jesus to be our Savior, the Holy Spirit comes to dwell in us (dwelling is **<u>active</u>**, a constant living within). *"And now you Gentiles have also heard the truth, the Good News that God saves you. And when you believed in Christ, He identified you as His own by giving you the Holy Spirit, whom He promised long ago. The Spirit is God's guarantee that He will give us the inheritance He promised and that He has purchased us to be His own people. He did this so we would praise and glorify Him."* **[Eph. 1:13-14]** *"Giving you the Holy Spirit"* in the NLT is translated *"sealed you with the*

Holy Spirit" in the English Standard Version (ESV).

7. How can your faith be made stronger? Prayer, spending time in God's Word, memorizing it, talking to God, and doing what God's Word says—all help us know who God is, developing in us hearts that are devoted to Him in intimate relationship.

8. Write down the convictions and *unshakable unbreakables* you now have to help you during the times you will be tested in life. _____

_____
_____
_____
_____
_____
_____
_____
_____
_____
_____
_____
_____
_____
_____

9. Need the Holy Spirit? Have you ever asked Jesus to be your Savior? _____ If not, what has held you back from doing so? Discuss this with your group leader or another Christian

believer in your group. Write down what is holding you back.

_____
_____
_____
_____
_____
_____
_____
_____

Are you ready to let go of being the master of your own ship? Are you ready to give Jesus the wheel so he can direct your life and save you from your sins, becoming the source of joy in your life? Are you ready to have the Holy Spirit live within, changing your heart and giving you strength and direction? If so, there is no better time to pray for salvation through Christ than now. Jesus is waiting for you with open arms. *"For everyone who calls on the name of the LORD will be saved."* **[Romans 10:13]** Are you ready for the angels in heaven to throw a party in your honor? *"...there is joy in the presence of God's angels when even one sinner repents."* **[Luke 15:10]**

If you don't know how to pray, turn to appendix A at the back of this book and read aloud the **Prayer for Salvation**. As some would say, the steps are simple (choose to ask Jesus to be your Savior), but not easy (the decision to follow Jesus is one that is lived out each day. It is a self-sacrificing journey, but worth everything. It is life-changing both now and throughout eternity).

DIGGING IN – WEEK TWO – GROUP TIME

Man's Laws over God's????

You have now seen how Satan tried to kill Daniel, Shadrach, Meshach, and Abednego, but because they **stood tall**, Satan failed. (Read the entire, amazing story of Nebuchadnezzar to discover God's victory in changing Nebuchadnezzar's heart to one of a true believer! See **Daniel chapters 1-4**)

But Satan's most important battle lay ahead—the battle against God's Son—Jesus—the Christ—the seed God promised to Adam and Eve who would save mankind. By defeating Jesus, Satan would have had a major victory against God—by it, mankind would have been be doomed to live eternally without Him.

The Serpent . . . and a Promised Seed

Satan's first attempt to kill Jesus as a child at the hand of Herod, the evil ruler of Judea, failed. **(Matthew 2:16-18)** Satan then tried to lure Jesus into sinning by personally tempting Him over a forty day period in the desert, appealing to human appetites: physical, emotional, and the lust for power, wealth, and fame. No human had ever withstood such temptations; but Jesus, with a heart completely devoted to His Father, **stood tall** quoting Scripture's truths. Once more Satan failed.

Not one to give up, the master deceiver had another scheme. It was to use a majority of Jewish religious leaders to plot Jesus' assassination. Satan's hope? Jesus would falter under the attacks of these men and refuse to become the "sacrificial lamb" for mankind's sin.

How on earth would Satan accomplish this? His plan of deception was and still is so simple that we often miss it. He would appeal to the rationale (logic) of mankind, in this case the Jewish rabbis, and encourage those religious leaders to create laws and traditions that would take eyes, hearts, and minds off God and His truths, and this is exactly what the rabbis did. While probably beginning with the best of intentions, these men became prideful and hypocritical. What do I mean by being hypocritical? Acting as though one is better than others…pretending to be holy, virtuous, righteous, above accusation of ever sinning or wrongdoing…that is hypocritical.

To explain the rabbi's actions further, you need a little bit of history. To guide Israelites' lives, God gave Moses the Ten Commandments in the book of Exodus and an additional 603 commandments in the next four books of the Bible (the Torah in the

Hebrew Bible and the Pentateuch in The Christian version 1). *So in total, there were 613 commandments the Israelites were to obey!* [2]

God had several objectives in giving these *Mosaic laws* to the Israelites. Because there were no governmental laws such as we have today, God's commandments such as those on *Love and Brotherhood, Dietary Laws*, etc., provided for the health, safety, and welfare of the Israelites and others. Those on *God* and the *Torah* gave instruction on who God was, how to honor Him, and how to teach who He was. The 613 commandments had even a more important purpose, however, and that was to prove to mankind that <u>no</u> human would be able to follow all these laws perfectly—*that ALL were sinners and needed a SAVIOR,* and that, of course, would be Jesus.

I'm sure you'll agree that 613 commandments were more than enough to clarify and accomplish God's purposes. *But no!* Jewish religious leaders believed more clarification was necessary and began adding oral laws to God's written laws. These were passed down through the generations, and after the second Jewish temple was destroyed in 70 AD, Jewish rabbis and scribes claimed the Oral Laws were given to Moses at the same time as the Written Law. Called the *Oral Laws of Judaism,* these as well as rabbinic traditions and sayings were written down in a book called the Mishnah so as not to be forgotten! [3,4]

Over the years, thousands of laws and traditions were added to make *righteous living* possible, at least according to the religious leaders! And in the end, all of these additional laws were taught as being either equal to or surpassing God's commands.

Imagine anything man could think of as being equal to God's! ***OUCH***! And believe it or not, these laws and traditions are still being added to today!

LAWS... LAWS... LAWS... LAWS... LAWS LAWS... LAWS

Israelites were burdened by LAW

Jesus replaced the burden of LAW with grace.

Can you see how Satan appealed to the rationale of Jewish religious leaders, encouraging them to *improve* on God's commands? Just as that nasty serpent deceived Adam and Eve, essentially telling them they needed *more* and encouraging them to be a law unto themselves, Satan appealed to the Jewish leaders' rationale, pride, and desire for power, motivating them to *clarify and improve* God's commands so they could, in the end, dictate Israelite life. These leaders would, hundreds of years later, and thousands of rules and traditions later, use these laws to try to entrap Jesus and have Him killed.

With all this in mind, let's examine how Jesus **stood tall**, *using truth* to dismantle one of the first challenges by the Pharisees, exposing their ***hardened hearts*** and the ***hypocrites*** they were. It all began when these religious leaders approached Jesus and His disciples. Read **Matthew 15:1-2** and Mark **7:1-5** to find out what was said, and answer the following:

1. What did the Pharisees and teachers of religious laws ask Jesus? They asked Him why some of His disciples disobeyed traditions that had been upheld for years, including the tradition that required ceremonial handwashing. Note: ceremonial handwashing, that required washing hands before, during, and after a meal, was not required by Old Testament law, but was passed down as a tradition to first-century Jews by their elders.

2. Did Jesus directly address the question the Pharisees asked? No

To understand why Jesus answered this way, read **Matthew 15:3-11** and **Mark 7:6-13** with the understanding that one of the traditions rabbis honored was the vow of Corbin. By this vow, an Israelite promised to give a certain amount of money to the temple treasury.

3. What do you think many Israelites did instead of obeying God's commandment to honor their parents: *"Honor your father and mother. Then you will live a long, full life in the land the LORD your God is giving you."* ? [**Ex.20:12**]

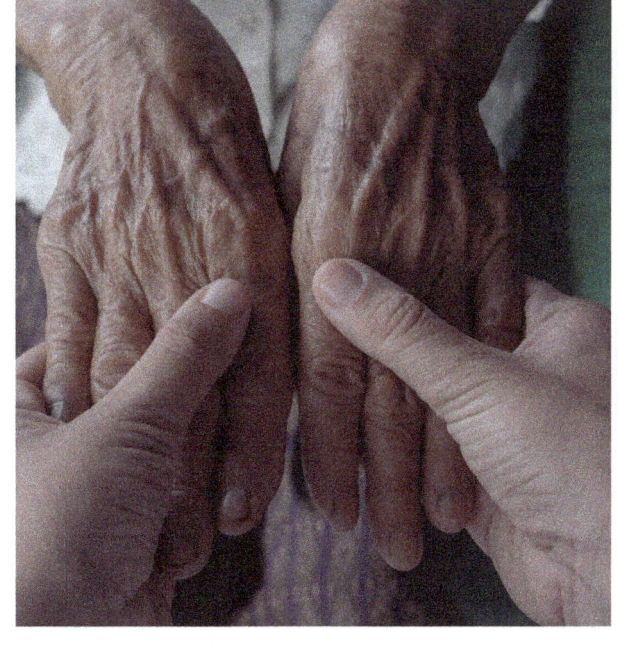

They took vows of Corbin so they would not have to support their parents. They were essentially saying, "I don't have money to support my parents because I have vowed my finances to the temple treasury." They were, therefore, in direct violation of God's command to honor their fathers and mothers not only as children, but throughout their parents' lives.

4. What did Jesus say was the result of this? The rabbis placed a man-made tradition above God's law, canceling His Word.

5. Why do you think the Jewish religious leaders created and allowed the vow of Corbin? Have students respond. Perhaps some wanted to ensure support of the temple, but others were greedy, wanting more money for themselves and the temple than otherwise would be given.

6. Did the Pharisees and teachers of the law urge honoring parents, showing empathy and concern for aging Jews? Did their actions display God's heart—His compassion, concern for, and all-consuming love for His people?

No, and this was truly a heart issue. The teachers of religious laws and Pharisees made evident their self-centeredness when they allowed the vow of Corbin to surpass God's loving commandment for children to honor their parents.

7. Why do you think God wrote the fifth commandment? Elicit teen opinions. Some might include that God is love, and He wants people of all ages then and now to be honored and provided for; God knows the problems of aging and has a plan for us to care for one another throughout our lives; God asks us to love as He loves, and that is sacrificially; also, by learning to honor parents, children will hopefully learn to honor God.

"Listening, respecting, and obeying are all implicit in the concept of honor. So is the dimension of support for needy parents that occasioned Jesus' rebuke of legalists (see glossary) *who resorted to Corban to withhold such support."* 5

Immediately after His reply to the Pharisees and lawmakers, Jesus pointed out their hypocrisy by addressing the handwashing issue. Jesus knew that God's definition of cleanliness and holiness meant an inward purity of heart; it was what was inside that counted, not what was on the outside. *"Jesus is saying pollution and defilement is not a physical issue, it is a spiritual one. It is not a ritual matter, it is a moral one... Now, at this juncture - and you want to understand this - He (Jesus) came to proclaim the truth that was inward, and they (the religious leaders) were completely committed to that which was outward religion."* John F. McArthur, Jr. 6 So Jesus stressed that it was not food touched by dirty hands that make people impure, defiling them, but the words they speak.

Read **Matthew 15:10-23**. Note verses 16-20: *"Don't you understand yet?" Jesus asked. "Anything you eat passes through the stomach and then goes into the sewer. But the words you speak come from the heart— that's what defiles you. For from the heart come evil thoughts, murder, adultery, all sexual immorality, theft, lying, and slander. These are what defile you. Eating with unwashed hands will never defile you."*

Jesus was and is always concerned with our hearts! By addressing God's fifth commandment in conjunction with ceremonial hand cleansing, Jesus revealed the sinful, hardened hearts of the Pharisees and the hypocrisy of their words.

"*Then the disciples came to Him (Jesus) and asked, 'Do you realize you offended the Pharisees by what you just said?'*" **[Matthew 15:13]** Did they Pharisees understand this? ***Absolutely***, for Jesus did not beat around the bush when He responded to them. Read some of His words in gospels other than Matthew:

"*You hypocrites! Isaiah was right when he prophesied about you, for he wrote, 'These people honor me with their lips, but their hearts are far from me.'*" **[Mark 7:6-]**

"*You skillfully sidestep God's law…*" **[Mark 7:9]**

"*You let them disregard…*" **[Mark 7:12]**

"*And so you cancel the Word of God in order to pass down your own tradition. And this is only one example among many others.*" **[Mark 7:13]**

No, when it came to truth, Jesus was a straight shooter—He spoke the truth because it needed to be spoken. True, his tone of voice varied depending upon the circumstances, such as when He spoke with gentleness and kindness to the Samaritan woman at the well, the woman who had committed adultery, and Nicodemus. But He spoke equally with passion and justified anger when others spoke or acted hypocritically, e.g. with the scribes and Pharisees, the moneychangers in the temple, etc.

In contrast with the Pharisees who placed burden after burden upon the shoulders of the Jews, Jesus' sought to remove that burden. His goal was and always will be to set His followers free. *"So Christ has truly set us free* (from the eternal penalty of sin). *Now make sure that you stay free, and don't get tied up again in slavery to the law."* **[Galatians 5:1]** He wants our hearts, minds, and bodies to be obedient to God's laws, not just externally to man's: *"The point is that Yeshua sets us free to become the children of God, not followers of the traditions of men…"* John J. Parsons 7

Rather than man's laws, Jesus always lived according to His Father's laws, His life modeling God's understanding, compassion, and love—a love so overwhelmingly great that in order to save sinners, Jesus was crucified. His desire for us is the same—that we love, honor, and glorify God the Father and love one another as deeply and clearly as He loved and continues to love **us.** Help teens sum up this lesson. How did Jesus **stand tall** against the religious leaders of His time? Ideas: Jesus knew Scripture and used the truth to refute their hypocrisy and lies, and His compassionate acts with those hurting physically and spiritually exemplified His loving heart.

Personal Time – Week Two – Day One

Jesus **stood tall** when it came to *legalism* versus *the heart*. To Him, obedience to His Father accompanied by love, mercy, grace, and compassion always prevailed over arbitrary manmade laws. For instance, Jewish religious leaders tried to clarify God's commandment to rest on the Sabbath by creating thirty-nine categories of prohibited work, each having subcategories: sowing, reaping, binding sheaves, threshing, winnowing, selecting, grinding, sifting, kneading, baking, shearing wool, washing wool, beating wool, dyeing wool, spinning, weaving, making two loops, weaving two threads, separating two threads, tying, untying, sewing stiches, tearing, trapping, slaughtering, flaying, tanning, scraping hide, marking hides, cutting hide to shape, writing two or more letters, erasing two or more letters, building, demolishing, extinguishing a fire, kindling a fire, the final hammer blow to finish newly made products, and carrying from the private to the public domain or vice versa.8 As an example of a subcategory, straightening a child's body or setting a broken limb broke Sabbath law.

Based on the above, explain what "laws" the Pharisees accused Jesus of breaking and how their challenges demonstrated their hardness of heart, especially relating to what Jesus identified as the two most important commandments, **loving God** (commandments 1-4) and **loving people** (commandments 5-10).

1. **John 5:8** *"Stand up, pick up your mat, and walk!"* In an act of compassion and love, Jesus healed a man who physically and spiritually broken by sin. Being healed, the man rolled up his

sleeping mat and began walking as Jesus had commanded, but the Pharisees were angered by this—both the man and Jesus were working on the Sabbath! Attacking the two, the Pharisees showed their total lack of understanding of God's commandments and His heart of loving compassion.

Furthermore, when the Pharisees accused Jesus of breaking Sabbath law because of the healing and Jesus replied that as His Father was always working, so was He, they knew Jesus was calling Himself equal to God. They were so concerned with *self* that, even though they thoroughly knew Scripture, they refused to recognize Jesus as the Messiah.

. **Matthew 2:1-2** *"At about that time Jesus was walking through some grain fields on the Sabbath. His disciples were hungry, so they began breaking off some heads of grain and eating them. But some Pharisees saw them do it and protested, 'Look, your disciples are breaking the law by harvesting grain on the Sabbath.'"* Again, the Pharisees accused Jesus of breaking Sabbath law. They did not care that Jesus' disciples were hungry, even though God did! In their eyes, Jesus' disciples were breaking two Sabbath prohibitions: first, they were, in a sense, reaping; second, they were winnowing by blowing on the grains, removing the chaff in order to eat the grain.

Would the Pharisees have done something similar if they had been hungry? I'm certain they would have, but being in the position that they were, they didn't have to worry about going without meals!

3. Based upon the above and **Matthew 15:8-9,** where Jesus said,

"These people honor me with their lips, but their hearts are far from me. Their worship is a farce, for they teach man-made ideas as commands from God," how does Jesus point out the hypocrisy of the Pharisees and Scribes? For each attack made upon Jesus, He responded with an example from Scripture that countered the accusation.

An example of this is when Jesus' disciples ate the grains of wheat. Jesus pointed out that David and his men ate consecrated bread when they were hungry, which went far beyond winnowing. *"Winnowing in order to eat when you're hungry is not violating God's Sabbath instructions. And neither the Sabbath nor the Holy Place is meant to deprive us of sustenance. Jesus was drawing the line between God's instruction and what the Rabbis had added to them."*9

Jesus understood what God really meant by keeping the Sabbath day holy. Since *holy* means being set apart, God wanted the Israelites to set apart the Sabbath day to put God first—to worship Him, glorify Him, and rest in Him. Worship means more than honoring or showing reverence to God by showing up at church, or in Jesus' day, to the temple. It means a lifestyle of living for the Lord every moment— placing Him first at all times. This is what Jesus did. In performing the miracles He did on the Sabbath, He was worshipping His Father by placing love, concern, compassion, and respect of others as an utmost priority. (For Old Testament verses on loving neighbors, see Leviticus, Chapter 19.) The Jewish religious leaders, however, taught the Jews to follow their rabbinical laws, which many times excluded demonstrating true love for one another.

A Child Demonstrates True Love--God's Heart

Does this kind of thing happen today? Yes! Sadly, here is an example from my life when I was about nine years old.

As I pointed out earlier, my family did not go to church regularly (or at all), but they did send me to a local church with legalistic laws. We were taught that eating meat on Fridays was a mortal sin, the punishment for which was eternity in hell. We were taught that sins could only be forgiven by confessing to a priest, whereby penance—a repetition of certain prayers—would be assigned for the forgiveness of those sins.

My parents played Bridge at their golf club every Friday night, and our family would have dinner there beforehand, kids eating separately from adults. The only meatless choice on the menu for me was a tuna fish sandwich. These tasted ***terrible,*** but week after week, I ate them, and Friday after Friday, I complained. My parents finally told me to have a hamburger instead. I did so, but then suffered from such a guilty conscience, I couldn't wait for Sunday to go to confession before church. When I confessed to the priest what I had done, he used scathing words, scolding me fiercely, declaring that if I had died before that Sunday, I would be in hell. He scared me to tears!!!

I look back on that event in life, and it really breaks my heart. Clearly, not eating meat on Fridays was a manmade law, and clearly, God never commanded that in His Word. Yet as a small girl, I was terrified that I would have gone to hell if I'd died because I ate that hamburger! How Pharisee-like could a law get?

We must learn from Jesus' example that knowing God's Word is vital. It teaches us how to respond to lies; it teaches who He is—of His sacrificial love, how and why we should love Him wholeheartedly in return, and how we should love others. This is exemplified through Jesus' life and example. How wonderful it is when our hearts are set on God!

5. Do you know of any pastors, religions, churches, or cults that make up their own manmade laws? If so, write what you know about these. Lead a discussion during Personal Group Discussion, asking if teens know of any instances of this. _____
_____
_____

5. Are these laws placed above God's laws and commandments? _____ Do they demonstrate God's heart and love for people? Explain why you do or do not believe these to be right or wrong. _____

Personal Time – Week Two – Day Two

1. After learning what Jesus taught regarding God's laws versus man-made laws, is there something in your life you should change to better follow Jesus and have a heart like His? If so, identify it and tell why you would want to change. _____

_____
_____
_____
_____
_____
_____
_____
_____
_____
_____
_____

2. Do you have any friends you feel are living under manmade laws rather than God's? Do you think you should discuss what you've learned with them? Explain why or why not. _____

_____
_____
_____
_____
_____

_____
_____
_____
_____
_____

3. Do you know of anyone who lives or speaks hypocritically, saying one thing while doing another, as if wearing a mask in one situation and taking it off in another?

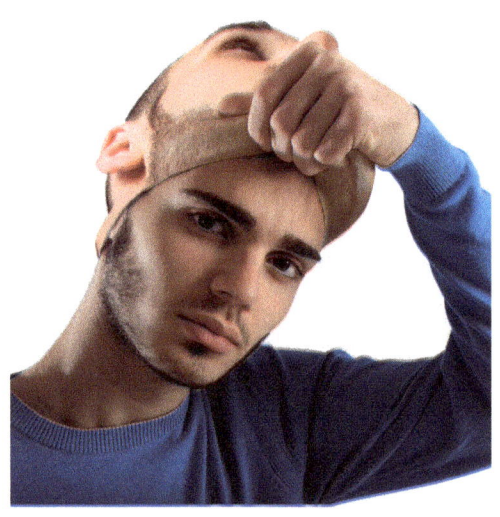

Without identifying these people (or person), describe how their words and/or actions differ and whether or not they demonstrate a hardness of heart. Explain how they either do or don't follow God's commandments to love Him with all their hearts, souls, and minds and love others as themselves. _____

_____
_____

Personal Time – Week Two – Day Three

The fourth commandment says to keep the Sabbath day holy. Consider our modern world. Many times sporting events (football, baseball, soccer, etc.) and other activities (e.g. dancing, theater, chess tournaments, etc.) are held on Sundays, and perhaps you participate in such activities as these. What does "Keep the Sabbath day holy" mean to you personally? How would you reply to someone who tells you that you should not participate in these things on Sundays but be in church, instead? This is a great topic for discussing the pros and cons of missing church. For some good discussion points, read the short article "Spring Sports and Sunday Church—Five Suggestions for Parents," an article by Tony Reinke, senior writer for Desiring God.[10] In this article, Tony relates the wisdom of Mary Kassain, a well-known author and speaker whose father-in-law played professional hockey, whose sons are athletes (one played professionally in the NHL), and whose husband is a bi-vocational pastor.[10] Ideas from another article with a slightly different twist is presented by Steve Turley in "Sports on Sundays: the Consequences of Skipping Church" in which he advocates for no Sunday morning sports.[11]

Personal Time – Week Two – Day Four

Many Jews used the Corbin vow as an excuse to get out of doing what they did not want to do, in spite of what God commanded. Think about your life. Have you ever done a similar thing (without the vow, of course), giving reasons for not doing something you did not want to do when you knew in your heart what God really desired/commanded? In other words, have you been hypocritical? In what state was your heart when you did this? Explain. _____

_____
_____
_____
_____
_____
_____
_____

If you have always done what you should, even when you did not want to, what or who helped you to do this? In what state was your heart? _____

_____
_____
_____
_____
_____
_____
_____

DIGGING IN – WEEK THREE – GROUP TIME

THE BLIND LEADING THE BLIND
Standing Tall in the Face of Blind Leaders

Mateo was running late! Shoving between students in his haste, he rushed into study hall just before the bell rang and hurriedly sat by his friends, Marcus and Benjamin. Heaving a huge sigh, Mateo whispered, "Hey, what's up?"

"Shhhh…no talking for a bit." Marcus grinned. "I'm tutoring Benjamin in algebra!"

Mateo's face registered shock. Marcus had told him just the day before that he got a *"D"* in algebra the prior semester. "Oh, no!" he thought. "This is the *blind leading the blind*!"

Good heavens! That doesn't present a great visual, does it, and it gets even worse if you change the picture to teens blindly and unwarily following others who are blinded!

It's pretty obvious what *blind leading the blind* means. It's not a modern term, but probably originated somewhere between the years 800 – 200 BC.1 What we do know is that Jesus definitely used the phrase to illustrate the heart condition of the Jewish religious leaders, known as scribes, and the Pharisees.

Read the following passages in Matthew, when Jesus called a crowd to him; in Mark, when Jesus explained to His disciples what He meant by that same parable; and once more in Luke, when Jesus gave the Beatitudes:

Matthew 15:10-13 *"Then Jesus called to the crowd to come and hear. 'Listen,' He said, 'and try to understand. It's not what goes into your mouth that defiles you; you are defiled by the words that come out of your mouth.'*

Then the disciples came to Him

and asked, 'Do you realize you offended the Pharisees by what you just said?' Jesus replied, 'Every plant not planted by my heavenly Father will be uprooted, so ignore them. They are blind guides leading the

blind, and if one blind person guides another, they will both fall into a ditch.' " **Mark 7:18-23**

In the following verses Jesus explains how the Pharisees were hypocritical and blinded in the parable above.) " *'Don't you understand either?' He asked. 'Can't you see that the food you put into your body cannot defile you?* **Food doesn't go into your heart**, *but only passes through the stomach and then goes into the sewer.' (By saying this, He declared that every kind of food is acceptable in God's eyes.) And then He added, ' It is what comes from inside that defiles you.* **For from within, out of a person's heart,** *come evil thoughts, sexual immorality, theft, murder, adultery, greed, wickedness,*

deceit, lustful desires, envy, slander, pride, and foolishness. All these vile things come from within; they are what defile you.'"

Luke 6:39 *"Then Jesus gave the following illustration: 'Can one blind person lead another? Won't they both fall into a ditch?' "*

When the Bible repeats something more than once, you know God is really stressing the idea. So let's look at what Jesus is saying here.

To begin, Jesus knew the scribes, Pharisees, and most of the Jewish people of the Old Testament considered themselves to be children of God and righteous simply because they were offspring from the seed of Abraham. *" 'Our father is Abraham!' they declared."* **[John 8:39]** It was like being born into a club… like having royal status because of being born to a king and queen… like being a member of aristocracy because parents hold a title or are wealthy. Many of the Pharisees however, not being seeds planted by God, were blinded by pride, desire for power, and the status quo of their positions with the Romans; ***their hearts, then, displayed how they were defiled.***

John the Baptist addressed their blindness: *"Prove by the way you live that you have repented of your sins and turned to God. Don't just say to each other, 'We're safe, for we are descendants of Abraham.' That means nothing, for I tell you, God can create children of Abraham from these very stones. Even now the ax of God's judgment is poised, ready to sever the roots of the trees. Yes, every tree that does not produce good fruit will be chopped down and thrown into the fire."* **[Matthew 3:8-10]** And so did Jesus when they declared they were sons of Abraham: *"So if the Son sets you free, you are truly free. Yes, I realize that you are descendants of*

*Abraham. And yet some of you are trying to kill me because **there's no room in your hearts for my message.** I am telling you what I saw when I was with my Father. But you are following the advice of your father* (Satan)... *for if you were really the children of Abraham, you would follow his example"* **[John 8:36-39]**

Remember in the book of Matthew, Jesus told His disciples to ignore the blind teachings of the scribes and Pharisees...that His Father would uproot all those not planted by Him. **[Matthew 15:13]** Who were those who were planted by God? John the apostle and Paul make this clear: *"But to all who believed Him* (Jesus) *and accepted Him, He gave the right to become children of God."* **[John 1:12]**

"In the same way, 'Abraham believed God, and God counted him as righteous because of his faith.' The real children of Abraham, then, are those who put their faith in God. What's more, the Scriptures looked forward to this time when God would make the Gentiles right in His sight because of their faith. God proclaimed this good news to Abraham long ago when He said, 'All nations will be blessed through you.' So all who put their faith in Christ share the same blessing Abraham received because of his faith." **[Galatians 3:6-9]**

Blindly following Jewish written and oral laws, the Pharisees failed to demonstrate love, grace, mercy, compassion, or the **loving heart** of God toward others. Worse yet, even though they thoroughly knew the prophecies that were being fulfilled by Jesus, they refused to accept Him as their Messiah.

Jesus **stood tall** and minced no words when He described this blindness of the Pharisees to the crowds and His disciples.

Read **Matthew 23:1-34** to learn about this. Have teens read these verses aloud, then answer the questions below.

1. Based on verses 3 and 4, how were the scribes and the Pharisees hypocritical? They didn't practice what they preached, burdening the Jews with unbearable religious demands, a heavy yoke as opposed to the light yoke Jesus proposed, *"Take My yoke upon you. Let Me teach you, because I am **humble** and **gentle at heart**, and you will find rest for your souls. For My yoke is easy to bear, and the burden I give you is light."* **[Matthew 11:29-30]** Whereas the pride of the Pharisees and scribes caused their hearts to be hardened and their words and actions to be hypocritical, Jesus stressed His ***humbleness*** and ***gentleness of heart***. Twice God revealed that Jesus was His Son and how pleased He was with Jesus: *"But even as He spoke, a bright cloud overshadowed them, and a voice from the cloud said, "This is My dearly loved Son, who brings Me great joy. Listen to Him."* **[Matthew 17:5]** See also **Mark 9:7** and **Luke 9:35**.

2. In verses 5-8, how did these leaders show themselves prideful? To draw extra attention to themselves, they wore extra

wide prayer boxes and robes with extra-long tassels. They took seats of honor at banquet tables and in the synagogues. They loved to be called rabbi, when they should not have, as Jesus taught that all Jews were equal and there was only one true teacher, God.

3. Beginning with verses 13 and 14, Jesus directed His remarks to the scribes and Pharisees. Why did Jesus say that sorrow awaited them? They preached against Jesus and God's kingdom and did their best to prevent others, even new converts, from accepting Jesus as God's Son.

4. In verse 16, Jesus first called the Jewish religious leaders "blind guides." Why was this? They preached that the created is more important than the Creator. e.g. the gold in the Temple was more important than God who made the gold sacred; the gifts on the altar were more important than God who made the altar sacred, etc. *They blindly were preaching against God's heart.*

5. Review verse 23. How did the religious leaders show themselves blind and hypocritical? They took pride in tithing, even to one-tenth of their herbs, but they failed to show the more important aspects of *God's law and heart* such as *justice, mercy, and faith*.

6. In verse 24, Jesus raised His voice in accusation: *"Blind guides! You strain your water so you won't accidentally swallow a gnat, but you swallow a camel!"* What was Jesus saying? In this hyperbole (an exaggeration comparing two things), physically swallowing a

gnat wouldn't be fatal, but swallowing a camel would. The *camel* represented the prideful, arrogant, and hypocritical teachings of the religious leaders which demonstrated how blind they were to the truth of who Jesus was.

7. In verses 25 through 26, Jesus demonstrated His point through *dishwashing*. What was He saying? The "greedy, self-indulgent" Pharisees were blind to the wickedness inside them. They needed to repent in order to become clean *inside*. Then they would be clean outside, also.

8. Jesus compareed the outward appearance of the scribes and Pharisees with whitewashed tombs. Remembering the extra-large Scripture boxes and extra-long robe tassels of the religious leaders, describe what the Jewish people were supposed to think when they saw these men. Whitewashed tombs were beautiful to observe, and so were the extravagant outer garments of the religious leaders and Pharisees. Their beauty was supposed to be a reminder for the Jews to revere the authority, status, and *wisdom* of their leaders. However, the garments were merely outer coverings that could not reveal the inner heart condition of those leaders.

9. What was on the inside of the whitewashed tombs? The bones of dead people and all the impurities that go along with the decomposition of bodies.

10. How did the interior of the tombs compare with the hearts of the scribes and Pharisees? Their hearts were filled with decay and also, in this case, *"hypocrisy and lawlessness."* These religious

leaders were totally blinded to who they really were._____
_____
_____
_____

Read **Matthew 16:6-11**. These verses talk about the *yeast of the Pharisees*. What do you know about yeast, and what does Jesus mean by "beware of the yeast of the Pharisees and Sadducees"?

Take a few minutes to discuss this with the group. Here are some ideas: Yeast is commonly used in bread making. When a very small amount is mixed in with flour and sugar, it quickly feeds on that sugar and ends up permeating all of the dough, affecting the entire loaf. The yeast of the Pharisees and Sadducees, then, was their disbelief in Christ. They stirred up trouble by attacking Christ's deity, desiring their yeast to effectively permeate and negate the truths the Jews were clearly seeing! Jesus therefore warned the disciples not to *fall* for this yeast, but to think about their experiences with Him and comprehend who He was—the Son of God and Messiah.

John 12:36b states, *"Put your trust in the light while there is still time; then you will become children of light."* Jesus knew the disciples did not understand who He really was, which is revealed when they questioned for a second time where to get bread to feed the crowd of 4,000 (more counting women and children) who were listening to Jesus. **(Matthew 15:29-39)**

With your group, summarize this lesson on **standing tall** in the face of others who are hypocritical and blindly leading the blind. Lead the teen discussion. Jesus **stood tall** by knowing the truth of Scripture, and He determined the heart condition of those who were teaching based on their motives, words, and actions. We need to do the same, learning God's Word and knowing His truth. We must not blindly follow either church leaders or those in our country, but make a commitment and *unshakable unbreakable* to examine words of what we are being taught to see if they align with God's Word, His loving heart, and His commands. We must stand on God's Word, and His Word alone.

Personal Time – Week Three – Day One

Jesus said to ignore blind leaders who would lead others into ditches. Think about the leaders in your church.

1. How can you be certain they are not blindly leading you into a *ditch* of lies? Have the teens carefully compare their pastor's sermons with God's Word. Are they based solely upon Scripture, or are they based on popular cultural norms and beliefs? If sermons are not based totally upon Scripture, explain to the teens how following that teaching would be blindness on their part.

2. As a child I was taught that only priests could interpret the Bible. Do you think this was true?

Bible in Asian Dialect

No. God wants all people to study His Word in order to gain knowledge, wisdom, and love for Him. Knowing this, believers have translated at least a part of the Bible into thousands of languages. (FYI: According to 2020 Wycliff statistics, there are 3415 languages with some Scripture, 704 languages with a complete Bible,

1551 languages with a complete New Testament, and 1160 languages with some translated Bible portions.)2

3. Why would God want all people to have Bibles they can read in their own language? One of God's great desires is to develop a personal relationship with people. The Bible is God's direct communication to us—His greatest *love letter* to all. _____

_____
_____
_____
_____

4. Have you ever examined what was said in a sermon with Scripture? Why or why not? _____

_____
_____
_____
_____
_____
_____
_____
_____

5. Do you have any friends or leaders in the public arena who you are blindly following? If so, identify these people and note why you are following them. What do you think God would have you do? Ask teens to honestly think about the above questions, then answer them. If the youth are blindly following others, discuss ways to determine if those they are following are lovers of God and

His truths. Do they love God with all their hearts, minds, souls, and strength, and do their words, actions, lifestyle, and obedience to God's Word demonstrate these things? If not, should these friends and leaders continue to be followed? _____

_____
_____
_____
_____
_____
_____
_____
_____
_____
_____
_____
_____
_____
_____
_____
_____
_____
_____
_____
_____
_____
_____
_____
_____
_____

Personal Time – Week Three – Day Two

Jesus said that a plant not planted by His Father would be uprooted, and it was noted that some of the Jews felt they were *plants* because they were *children (descendants) of Abraham.*

Who Is Your Father? Who Planted You?

Are you a plant, one planted by the Father? In other words, if you say you are a Christian, are you really? Do you base your being a Christian because your parents are? Because you attend church on Sundays? Wednesdays? Youth group? Have you been baptized? If so, did you fully understand this did not mean salvation but was an indication that you were transferring the rights of your life over to Jesus? That He is now in command? That you must die to self to follow Him?

These questions require deep thought and reflection. Think about how your life and thoughts reveal either your commitment to follow Jesus or to satisfy your own desires. Pray and ask God to open your eyes to the truth about yourself, then write what He lays upon your heart. _____

_____

Personal Time – Week Three – Day Three

Read the following verses carefully.

- *"So if you ignore the least commandment and teach others to do the same, you will be called the least in the Kingdom of Heaven."* **[Matthew 5:19]**

- *"You have heard that our ancestors were told, 'You must not murder. If you commit murder, you are subject to judgment.' But I say, if you are even angry with someone, you are subject to judgment! If you call someone an idiot, you are in danger of being* 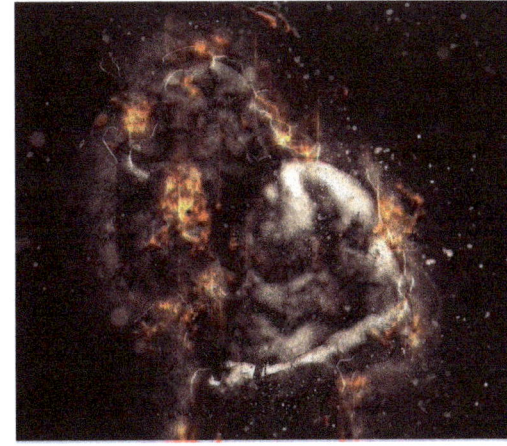 *brought before the court. And if you curse someone, you are in danger of the fires of hell."* **[Matthew 5:21-22]**

- *"Do not judge others, and you will not be judged. For you will be treated as you treat others. The standard you use in judging is the standard by which you will be judged."* **[Matthew 7:1-2]**

- *"Do to others as you would have them do to you. This is the essence of all that is taught in the law and the prophets.* **[Matthew 7:12]**

- *"Yes, just as you can identify a tree by its fruit, so you can identify people by their actions."* **[Matthew 7:20]**

Use the above verses to explain the blindness, hardness of heart, and hypocrisy of the scribes and Pharisees in the following two situations:

1. *"When they (the two healed blind men) left, a demon-possessed man who couldn't speak was brought to Jesus. So Jesus cast out the demon, and then the man began to speak. The crowds were amazed.*

'Nothing like this has ever happened in Israel!' they exclaimed. But the Pharisees said, 'He can cast out demons because He is empowered by the prince of demons.'" **[Matthew 9:34]** (See also **Matthew 12:23-24**; **Luke 11:15**; **Mark 3:22**) *Based on Matthew 7:1-2, the Pharisees were judging; and based on Matthew 7:12, they were treating others wrongfully.* The Pharisees cared nothing for the mute man who was healed. They only cared that Jesus was the healer and that He defied their authority by healing on the Sabbath. Far worse, they attributed Jesus' power to Satan, which blasphemed the Holy Spirit. Because of their hardened hearts, the Pharisees remained blinded to Jesus' divinity, even though they knew Scripture and the prophecies regarding the coming Messiah. An article by Focus on the Family states: *"By continually rejecting God's free gift of salvation in Jesus, a sinner sears his conscience (ignores the voice of the Holy Spirit) and stiffens his neck. Eventually, he gets to the place where genuine repentance is no longer possible. This*

stubborn and unrepentant attitude — persistent self-hardening — is the chief mark of true blasphemy against the Holy Spirit." 3

2. *"At about the same time, Jesus was walking through the grain fields on the sabbath. His disciples were hungry, so they began breaking off some heads of grain and eating them. But the Pharisees saw them do it and protested, 'Look, your disciples are breaking the law by harvesting grain on the sabbath.' "* When asked, Jesus repeated God's two most important commandments, to love the Lord with all their hearts, souls, minds, and strength and to love their neighbors as themselves. **(Mark 12:30)** So many times the Pharisees did not *love their neighbor as themselves*, for in this instance they would have demanded Jesus' disciples to go hungry—definitely something God would never desire! **[Matthew 22:39]** To counter their attack, Jesus pointed out two examples from the Scriptures: David's hungry men ate the priests' sacred loaves of bread; and the priests worked in the Temple on the Sabbath, as allowed by Moses. In an allusion to Himself, Jesus said He was greater than the Temple and that the Pharisees would not accuse His disciples of sinning had the Pharisees understood the meaning of *"I want you to show mercy, not offer sacrifices."* **(Hosea 6:6)** Hosea **6:6** furthermore ends with, *"I want you to know Me more than burnt offerings."* In a similar fashion, Jesus desires that the Pharisees recognize Him as the Son of God, for He states, *"For the Son of Man is Lord, even over the Sabbath."*

3. Why did the scribes and Pharisees become hypocritical blind men? Sum up what you have learned so far, using the following verses as guides: *"Guard your heart above all else, for it determines the*

course of your life." **[Proverbs 4:23]** *"A good person produces good things from the treasury of a good heart, and an evil person produces evil things from the treasury of an evil heart. What you say flows from what is in your heart."* **[Luke 6:45]**

The scribes and Pharisees were prideful, arrogant, desired power, wanted to keep their positions with the Romans, and cared about their own laws and traditions more than about loving others as themselves, as God desired. Their hardened hearts blinded them to being compassionate, loving others in need, and recognizing Jesus as the Messiah.

What does your heart's treasury hold?

Personal Time – Week Three – Day Four

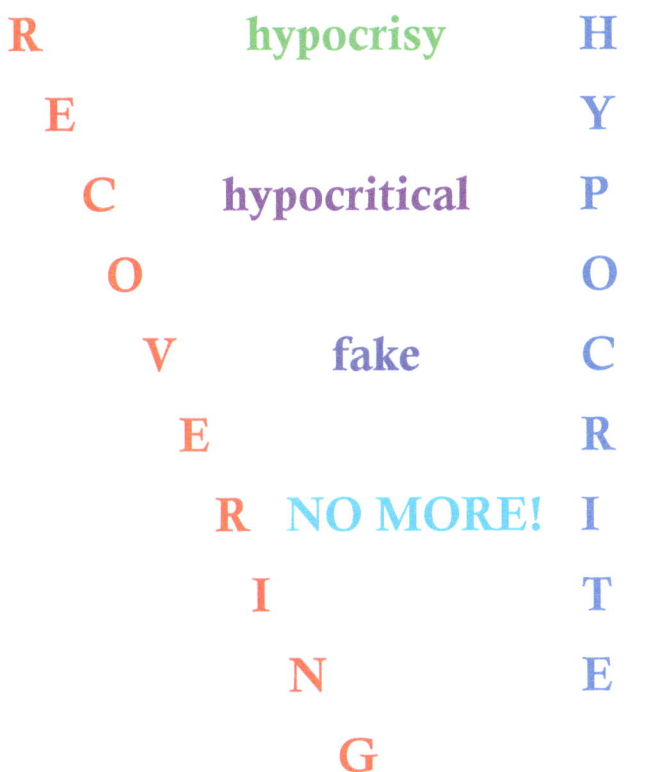

In exploring the internet, I've come across the term, *recovering hypocrite* quite a few times. Being hypocritical…we've all acted this way at one time or another, because being open about who we really are makes us vulnerable in the eyes of others. We place what people think above what God thinks. ***This is wrong!*** God should always be first in our lives! When our focus is on Him, we don't need to be afraid of what others think of us because there is no shame and "*…no condemnation for those who belong to Christ Jesus.*" [**Romans 8:1**] We can **stand tall**!

Perhaps we are a *recovering blind person*, having followed a blind leader, not comparing that person's words with their actions, but now we know better. So here is the question: Are you *in recovery?* Have you ever acted in a hypocritical manner and/or blindly followed someone? I have, Terry has, and sadly, here's an example.

A Terry and Candice Story:

It was May of 1986, an election year. Terry and I were introduced to a former pastor turned politician who was running against an incumbent who supported abortion. After being introduced to the former pastor and wife, having several meals with them, learning of his pro-family and pro-life stances, we became supporters of his campaign. We were so excited…a pastor, a man of God…what better person to elect as a United States senator in our country?

This man lost the election. Much more to our dismay, however, was the fact after the election, it was discovered that he had been having an affair with one of his staffers. He ended up divorcing his wife and leaving his children.

Terry and I were heart-broken. How could a former man of God and a person who proclaimed love for his family and for unborn children do such a thing? And how could we have known his true character?

This would have been difficult, but perhaps by talking to his wife separately and contacting his former church, Terry and I would have learned more about his character before supporting him. We know now we should have done more to discern this man's true character before blindly leading others to follow him.

Your Turn:

Pray for a few minutes, take a deep breath, and ask God to open your eyes to any time you may have acted hypocritically and/or have blindly followed someone. Be very honest with yourself. Now write what God has revealed to you. _____

_____
_____
_____
_____
_____
_____
_____

Based upon what you have written, are you now *in recovery*? If so, what helped you recognize that you needed to act genuinely and/or quit following someone? _____

_____
_____
_____
_____
_____

DIGGING IN – WEEK FOUR – GROUP TIME
Jesus Stood Tall Regarding Marriage

Marriage, what a **HUGE** topic! Indeed, it is one of the most important topics you *will* face in your lifetime. Are you called to be married (yes, it is a calling—that divine purpose God has designed for your life), or are you called to be single? Only you and God can know. You'll need to spend much time together in prayer to determine this, with you listening for God's voice and the inner peace He will give you regarding your decision.

A fact you should recognize is that all who marry are sinners, so in marriage, one sinner is marrying another. I'll be the first to admit I never once thought, *"I'm so excited! I'm going to marry the one I love, my best friend, and my very own sinner!"* The *sinning* part never entered my mind! However, based on this truth, it is guaranteed that when sinners live together, there will be a time of differences and difficulties.

Before marrying, then, you need to be certain that as many obstacles as possible to a successful marriage are removed and that you have the ability to communicate well with the other person.

First, let's look at what Jesus said about marriage and go from there. Read **Matthew 19:1-9** and **Matthew 5:32**.

1. What was Jesus doing at this time? He was east of the Jordan River in Judea, interacting with large crowds and healing the sick.

2. Who walked up to Jesus to challenge Him, and what did they ask? The Pharisees. They asked, *"Should a man be allowed to divorce his wife **for just any reason**?"*

To this Jesus replies, *" 'Haven't you read the Scriptures?... They record that from the beginning God made them male and female. And He said, 'This explains why a man leaves his father and mother and is joined to his wife, and the two are united into one. Since they are no longer two but one, let no one split apart what God has joined together.' "* **[Matthew 19:4-6]**

Jesus had gone to the very heart of the issue. ***What is marriage?*** Let's read together God's Word in **Genesis 2:18-23**:

*"Then the L*ORD *God said, '**It is not good for the man to be alone**. I will make a **helper** who is just right for him.' So the L*ORD *God formed from the ground all the wild animals and all the birds of the sky.*

He brought them to the man to see what he would call them, and the man chose a name for each one. He gave names to all the livestock, all the birds of the sky, and all the wild animals.

But still there was no helper just right for him. *So the* LORD *God caused the man to fall into a deep sleep. While the man slept, the* LORD *God took out one of the man's ribs and closed up the opening. Then the* LORD *God made a woman from the rib, and He brought her to the man.*

'At last!' the man exclaimed. 'This one is bone from my bone, and flesh from my flesh! She will be called woman, because she was taken from man.'"

Remember how in **Genesis 1**, God stated that everything was ***good***, and when He concluded creation, He stated that everything was ***very good***. But in **Genesis 2**, for the first time we read that God Himself said something ***was not good***. **[Genesis 2:18]** Our all-knowing God said that for our benefit. Let's see why.

3. What was not good? It was not good for Adam to be alone.

4. What then did God create? All animals.

5. Were any of them *"just right"* for Adam? No Why? No animal would be adequate to function as Adam's helper, for only man was made in God's image and the only creation in whom God breathed His breath of Life. *"Genesis 2:7 tells us that man became a living soul (KJV). The word soul in Hebrew is **nephesh**, meaning an animated, breathing, conscious, and living being. Man did not become a living soul until God breathed life into him. As a physical animate, rational, and spiritual being, man is unique among all living things upon the earth…"* [1]

What Adam needed was a corresponding human helper, one also made in God's image; one who would provide a relationship that would differ from all other male/female pairs by being personal, intimate, permanent, and complementary (completing).

6. How did God create Adam **(Genesis 2:7)**, and how did He create Eve? God created Adam out of the dust of the ground; He created Eve from one of Adam's ribs.

7. What was Adam's response to Eve's creation? He was exultant and overjoyed! He named Eve *woman* because he was *man*, and she was created from part of him.

Eve was literally created from a part of Adam! They truly were one, exemplifying God's design for marriage: ***"This explains why a man leaves his father and mother and is joined to his wife, and <u>the two are united into one</u>."*** **[Genesis 2:24]**

Marriage was designed by the Father as a ***one man, one woman, one union, and one flesh relationship.***

As a 2-part jigsaw puzzle, husband and wife join together as one.

The Pharisees then continued to question Jesus. " 'Then why did Moses say in the law that a man could give his wife a written notice of divorce and send her away?' they asked.

Jesus replied, 'Moses permitted divorce only as a concession to your hard hearts, but it was not what God had originally intended. And I tell you this, whoever divorces his wife and marries someone else commits adultery—unless his wife has been unfaithful.' " **[Matthew 19:7-9] [Matthew 5:32] [Luke 16:19] [Mark 10:10-12]**

Powerful words of God delivered by His Son, Jesus, demonstrated that divorce should not be the norm. Marriage was to be **a lifelong commitment—a covenant** between a man and woman *"from this day forward, for better, for worse, for richer, for poorer, in sickness and in health, to love and to cherish, till death do us part, according to God's holy ordinance; and thereto I pledge thee my faith to you."* 2

With all this being said, if you one day feel God is calling you to marry (and that is probably many years off), before you propose to someone or accept a proposal, you need to carefully and honestly examine *who you are,* acknowledging your strengths and weaknesses. You need to be certain you are *healthy* and you need to know *why* you want to marry, because marriage is *not about getting* something; it *is about giving* something, and that is *your all*. It is about *servanthood*—giving one hundred percent to serve your mate, and your mate giving one hundred percent to serve you. It's about putting the needs of the other first and foremost in all you do, each day and every day:

"But among you (my disciples) it will be different. Whoever wants to be a leader among you must be your servant, and whoever wants to be first among you must become your slave. ***For even the Son of Man came not to***

be served but to serve others and to give his life as a ransom for many." [Matthew 20:26–28] [Mark 10:35–45]

AM I HEALTHY?

Let's examine being *healthy* in further detail. This is good to do now, but it is essential to do before marriage. Ask a ***trusted***, yet ***honest***, friend to help you answer the following questions slowly and deliberately:

- Am I a promise keeper? Do I keep my word even in the smallest of matters? Does my "yes" mean "yes" and my "no", "no"?
- Do I struggle with anger, alcohol, depression, drugs, pornography, selfishness, stubbornness, a need always to be right, self-loathing, an abusive nature toward animals or others, bullying, gambling, or gaming?
- Do I communicate with kind, thoughtful words or withdraw and give the "silent treatment" when I feel challenged, criticized, neglected, or even when complimented?
- Will I commit now to counseling and/or treatment if I struggle with any of the above issues? Why or why not?
- Before marriage, will I commit to seek premarital counseling by a godly pastor, which includes the *Prepare and Enrich* compatibility study or another equally accurate evaluation to identify issues my future mate and I might have in order to strengthen prospects for a successful marriage?
- Will I now pledge to obtain Christian counseling if my spouse

or I experience and/or express ongoing difficulties in our marriage? Discuss the meaning and importance of each issue.

To examine yourself in such a manner demands **standing tall**; however, these questions are vital, and you'll need to ask them not only of yourself but of the one you someday choose to marry. If you display any of the above personal issues, they need to be resolved before marriage. Problems tend to grow as a result of daily living, even with those we love.

There is another vital question to ask yourself before marriage: ***"Why am I choosing to get married?"*** Is it because you want to get out of a bad situation in your home? Feel lonely? Need to feel loved? Valued? These are dangerous reasons to marry…and there are so many, many more.

Why is this dangerous? You are basing marriage on *what it can give you*, allowing you to walk away if you feel your emotional or romantic needs are not met. This is not God's plan! He designed marriage as a covenant—a binding, lifelong relationship that places that covenant far above personal needs. ***<u>In other words, the covenant becomes the foundation of, and therefore the security in, your marriage</u>***.

Each spouse in marriage, then, gives one hundred percent of self to the other. It is never, "I've done my fifty percent; now do yours." Husband and wife are to complete, not deplete, one another, and this takes daily, selfless, sacrificial love and purposely places the needs of the other before the needs of self.

Our perfect example is Jesus.

8. Look up **Matthew 20:28** and **Mark 10:45** and write what it is that Jesus teaches us. He teaches us to serve rather than be served and to sacrificially give our lives for the sake of others.

9. What does Jesus say in **Matthew 20:16**? Those who are last will be first, and those who are first will be last. We should place our spouse's desires and needs first in our married journey together through life.

10. Read **1 Corinthians 13:4-5**. What does a self-sacrificial love look like? It is patient, kind, does not envy or boast, and it isn't proud. It does not dishonor others *and is not self-seeking*. It isn't easily angered and keeps no record of wrongs. Discuss each of the above in detail.

11. **John** teaches us in verse **15:13** that *"there is no greater love than to lay down one's life for one's friends."* And Jesus says, *"If any of you wants to be my follower, you must give up your own way, take up your cross daily, and follow me,"* which, as we learned, means total **standing tall servanthood**. How would you apply these verses to marriage? Humans are, by nature, self-centered. Placing our spouse and his/her needs before our own does require self-sacrificial love. Sacrificing on a regular, daily basis can be difficult, and it may demonstrate one of the ways we die to self and carry our cross.

To summarize, marriage is a covenant in which a man and woman vow to weather every storm, consistently support one another, and to sacrificially and selflessly love each other. William

Shakespeare beautifully defines what love looks like when built on such a covenant foundation: Sonnet 116 *"Let me not to the marriage of true minds admit impediments. Love is not love which alters it when alteration finds, or bends with the remover to remove: O no! It is an ever fixed mark that looks on tempests and is never shaken; it is the star to every wandering bark whose worth's unknown, although his height be taken. Love's not Time's fool, though rosy lips and cheeks within his bending sickle's compass come: Love alters not with his brief hours and weeks, but bears it out, even to the edge of doom."* 3

If you and your future spouse pledge to do all the above, you will not have to worry about divorce, the topic addressed to Jesus by the Pharisees. Instead, keeping in mind that the foundation of marriage is your covenant—and that your covenant is based on servanthood—your love will flourish, blossoming into the most beautiful image you can imagine: *"As you gave the ring to one another and have now received it a second time from the hand of the pastor, so love comes from you, but marriage from above, from God. As high as God is above man, so high are the sanctity, the rights, and the promise of love. It is not your love that sustains the marriage, but from now on, the marriage that sustains your love."* — Dietrich Bonhoeffer, Letters and Papers from Prison 4

COVENANT . . .

AN UNBREAKABLE

PROMISE

Personal Time – Week Four – Day One

Take a few minutes to pray to your heavenly Father, asking Him to take away any false assumptions you have about yourself and to clearly see truth. Then, take the following assessment. If a close, trusted friend can be with you as you do this, that's all the better. If not, at some point, meet with this friend to go over your assessment and gather honest input to your answers.

SELF-EVALUATION

1. I believe I have the following strengths that would benefit a spouse in marriage: _____

_____
_____
_____
_____
_____
_____
_____
_____
_____
_____
_____

Discuss what the teens have written. Please add to these your personal thoughts.

2. These are some issues I see in myself that I will work on improving and/or receive counseling before marriage: _____

_____
_____
_____
_____
_____
_____
_____
_____
_____
_____
_____
_____
_____
_____
_____
_____
_____
_____
_____
_____
_____
_____
_____

Again, discuss and add your personal thoughts.

3. I admit that I struggle with the following:

ANGER _____ Yes _____ No   Example: _____

_____
_____
_____
_____

ALCOHOLISM _____ Yes _____ No   Example: _____

_____
_____
_____
_____

DEPRESSION _____ Yes _____ No   Example: _____

_____
_____
_____
_____

DRUGS _____ Yes _____ No   Example: _____

_____
_____
_____
_____

PORNOGRAPHY _____ Yes _____ No   Example: _____

_____
_____

SELFISHNESS _____ Yes _____ No Example: _____

STUBBORNNESS _____ Yes _____ No Example: _____

A NEED ALWAYS TO BE RIGHT _____ Yes _____ No
Example: _____

SELF-LOATHING _____ Yes _____ No Example: _____

AN ABUSIVE NATURE TOWARD ANIMALS/OTHERS OR VICTIM OF SEXUAL/EMOTIONAL/PHYSICAL ABUSE____

Yes ____ No   Example: _____

_____

_____

_____

BULLYING ____ Yes ____ No   Example: _____

_____

_____

_____

GAMBLING ____ Yes ____ No   Example: _____

_____

_____

_____

GAMING ____ Yes ____ No   Example: _____

_____

_____

_____

Carefully examine your *yes* answers above. Have you and/or your friend identified areas indicating you need help either through counseling or rehab for you to become *healthy* and godly like Jesus? I know it's probably a scary thought, but if so, *please* be open to getting help…*now* is always better than later. Contact your small group leader or another adult you trust who will guide you to appropriate help. Review signs of each problem. Prepare handouts listing resources to help teens resolve their issues.

Ideas: Pastors, school counselors, National Non Profit Helpline, a 24/7, 365-day-a-year treatment referral and information service for individuals and families faced with mental and/or substance use disorders: 1-877-882-9275 .

Personal Time – Week Four – Day Two

Communication Skills

If you have trouble communicating now, your lack of skill will only grow worse in marriage. With this in mind, please write down how you communicate with others. For example, do you

use use words to solve differences or conflicts, or do you withdraw, running or walking from a room? Do you scream or use a controlled tone of voice? Do you give the "silent treatment" by not talking when you feel challenged, criticized, neglected, or even when complimented? Do you internalize your thoughts or express them? Write your answer here. _____

_____

_____

_____

_____

_____
_____
_____
_____
_____
_____

Why do you think you communicate the way you do? What frustrations do you have in communicating and what triggers those frustrations. _____
_____
_____
_____
_____
_____
_____
_____
_____
_____

If you need help communicating more appropriately, ask your small group leader and/or a high school counselor to recommend resources with whom you might work.

Personal Time – Week Four – Day Three

Have you ever thought about marriage? If so, before this study did you understand that it is a calling from God, and have you considered praying about this? If not, would you consider doing so now and during future years? If "no," why not? _____

_____
_____
_____
_____
_____
_____

In the past, what did you feel marriage was based on? Be honest, even if it is…you know…that three letter word…*sex*! Explain what formed your opinion. _____

_____
_____

Have you ever considered that marriage is a self-sacrificing relationship? That you will be placing your spouse's needs above your own? What are your thoughts about this, and what are you willing to sacrifice?

Have you seen good examples of marriages? If so, what are the qualities you would like to imitate?

If you have thought about marriage, what are your hopes for it?

Personal Time – Week Four – Day Four

Paul penned the following words in a letter he wrote to the Christians in Corinth. That church was struggling with many issues, one of which he addresses in the following verses, given in several versions:

"Don't team up with those who are unbelievers. How can righteousness be a partner with wickedness? How can light live with darkness?" **[2 Corinthians 6:14] NLT**

"Do not be unequally yoked with unbelievers. For what partnership has righteousness with lawlessness? Or what fellowship has light with darkness?" **[2 Corinthians 6:14] ESV**

"Don't become partners with those who reject God. How can you make a partnership out of right and wrong? That's not partnership; that's war. Is light best friends with dark? Does Christ go strolling with the Devil?

Do trust and mistrust hold hands? Who would think of setting up pagan idols in God's holy Temple? But that is exactly what we are, each of us a temple in whom God lives. God Himself put it this way: 'I'll live in them, move into them; I'll be their God and they'll be my people. So leave the corruption and compromise; leave it for good," says God.

"Don't link up with those who will pollute you. I want you all for myself. I'll be a Father to you; you'll be sons and daughters to me.' **[2 Cor. 6:14-18]**
The Message Bible

Marriage—being yoked together. I'm sure by now you've at least seen a picture of yoked horses or oxen, working in unison to plow fields or pull wagons steadily, such as the covered wagons of yesteryear. Let's paint another picture. Visualize a covered wagon moving along the Oregon Trail pulled by pairs of horses and oxen, with one horse and one ox being yoked together in each pair. How does the picture look now? Is the ride smooth or bumpy? Do you think the different temperaments of each species might cause an issue with the other? You can bet on that!

The words of Paul make it very clear that when a believer becomes unequally yoked to a non-believer in marriage, the one who loves and honors God and wants to grow in Christ will suffer because of the non-acceptance and rejection of God's Son by the other. Disputes may arise over morality, how to raise children, time spent in church, Christian ministry, finances, support of the church and/or charities, etc. The two spouses will not function as one, but only as individuals who live in the same house, *pulling* forward at different speeds and in different directions. ***Not good!***

Knowing this, how important is it that when you start dating, you date only a Christian believer?

DIGGING IN—WEEK FIVE—GROUP TIME

Jesus Stands Tall Regarding Marriage—Part Two

Did Jesus **stand tall** regarding the sanctity of marriage? Last week we learned that He certainly did! Because His definition of marriage was so exacting and strong, I feel it is important for us to spend more time in God's Word, taking into the very core of our hearts God's design for that union. Let's review one more time what Jesus said in the following verses before examining other Scripture. Have teens read these aloud.

*"Then the LORD God said, 'It is **not good for the man to be alone**. I will make **a helper** who is just right for him.' So the LORD God formed from the ground all the wild animals and all the birds of the sky. He brought them to the man to see what he would call them, and the man chose a name for each one. He gave names to all the livestock, all the birds of the sky, and all the wild animals. **But still there was no helper just right for him.***

*So the LORD God caused the man to fall into a deep sleep. While the man slept, the LORD God took out one of the man's ribs and closed up the opening. **Then the LORD God made a woman from the rib, and He brought her to the man.***

*'At last!' the man exclaimed. 'This one is bone from my bone, and flesh from my flesh. She will be called woman, because she was taken from man.' **This explains why a man leaves his father and mother and is joined to his wife, and the two are united into one."*** **[Genesis 2:18-24]**

Again, we have *one man and one woman, covenanting to*

come together as one flesh, one union. Bride and groom clarify their covenant by saying vows in front of God and witnesses, and off they ride into the sunset to live happily ever after. Right? Oh, don't we wish this were a Cinderella story? Don't we long for that fairytale ending?

The beauty of this is, when a committed believer marries another committed believer, both with hearts devoted to God's Word, we can have this happy ending! Before that ending, however, understanding and growth must take place as each spouse grows in the Lord as an individual and together as a couple. Remember, sinner is marrying sinner, and at some point the road on their journey will become bumpy. For some  there may be a pothole or two, but for others there may be sinkholes, boulders, fallen trees, and entangled electrical lines impeding the road. Understanding and gaining wisdom from God's Word enables spouses to navigate over, around, and through these challenges.

Look up the following verses with your group, read them aloud, then discuss and summarize what God wants from you in marriage so the thought of divorce will never enter your mind:

Leaders, I will type these verses for you. Based on these verses, develop discussion with the teens.

1. **Hebrews 13:4** *"Give honor to marriage, and remain faithful to one another in marriage. God will surely judge people who are immoral and those who commit adultery."* I am to honor the foundation of marriage, upon which love builds. I am to remain faithful always, never to give thought to another. I might seldom give thought to God's reaction to sin, but it is true that He is just and will judge my immoral sins if I don't repent of them.

2. **Eph. 4:32** *"Instead, be kind to each other, tenderhearted, forgiving one another, just as God through Christ has forgiven you."* Forgiveness is one of the keys to a successful marriage. Because I am a sinner, as is my spouse, I am to practice forgiving not only seven times seven, but always. I am to be kind and tenderhearted toward my spouse, not keeping a record of wrongs, but again, always being ready to forgive.

3. **Eph. 4:2** *"Always be humble and gentle. Be patient with each other, making allowance for each other's faults because of your love."* Patience and humility are keys to a successful marriage. I must be patient with myself as I grow and patient with my spouse as he/she grows. I should never be prideful, feeling I am growing in Christ faster than my spouse or developing a deeper relationship with Jesus than he/she is. This holds true in every area of life. Again, I am to walk through life with humbleness, ever being thankful for my spouse.

4. **1 Cor. 13:4-8** *"Love is patient and kind. Love is not jealous or boastful or proud or rude. It does not demand its own way. It is not irritable,*

and it keeps no record of being wronged. It does not rejoice about injustice but rejoices whenever the truth wins out. Love never gives up, never loses faith, is always hopeful, and endures through every circumstance." These verses speak for themselves. True love is a heart condition—it is agape love—unconditional. Each spouse must place the physical and emotional needs of the other above self.

Leaders, spend some time with the teens delving into these

ideas. Are the teens able to identify instances of love either being carried out or not in the manner the verses describe? Be prepared to give your own examples.

Hearts devoted to God and His Word, leading you to be faithful, kind, tenderhearted, forgiving, humble, gentle, patient—not boasting or keeping records of wrongs, not demanding your own way, and never giving up—these all are characteristics of what God wants you to be in marriage. Pretty easy to understand, right? But what about the following passages regarding men's and women's roles in marriage?   In today's society, they readily cause dispute.

*"For **wives**, this means **submit to your husbands as to the Lord**. For a **husband is the head** of his wife as Christ is the head of the church. He is the Savior of His body, the church. As the church submits to Christ, so you wives should submit to your husbands in everything. **For husbands, this means love your wives, just as Christ loved the church**. He gave up His life for her to make her holy and clean, washed by the cleansing of God's Word. He did this to present her to Himself as a glorious church without a spot or wrinkle or any other blemish. Instead, she will be holy and without fault. In the same way, **husbands ought to love their wives as they love their own bodies**. For a man who loves his wife actually shows love for himself. No one hates his own body but feeds and cares for it, just as Christ cares for the church. And we are members of His body."* **[Ephesians 5:22-30]**

*"But there is one thing I want you to know: **The head of every man is Christ, the head of woman is man, and the head of Christ is God.**"* **[1 Corinthians 11:3]**

Why was it necessary for these apostles to clarify the issues of **headship**, **submission**, **and how men are to love their wives**--in other words, women's and men's roles in marriage? The simple answer… mankind's rebellion against God!

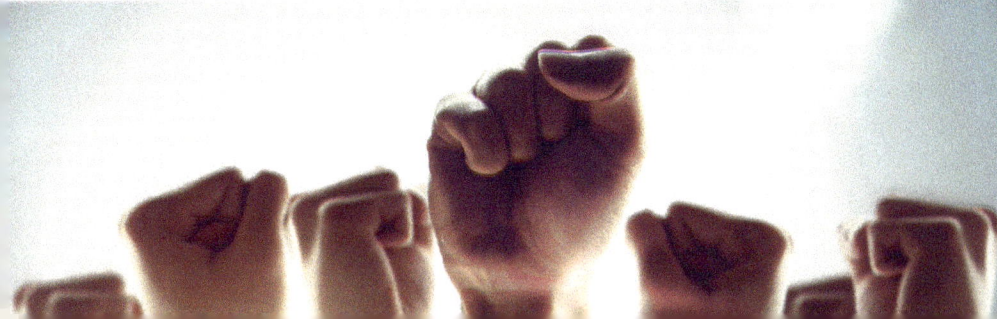

5. Describe the state of the world, animals, and men after God created all in **Genesis 1** and **2**. Everything was perfect.

6. Explain why Eve was created? She was created so Adam would not be alone but have a mate whose heart would be devoted to him as his **helper**, strengthening and complementing him.

As we move on in our study, it is *vital* to understand that while *helper* **implies** one who is inferior to another more studied in our culture, **it does not** in the Bible; rather, a helper *strengthens* the one being helped. Eve gave Adam *strength* in the areas he was lacking, and this is God's plan for you as a future wife.

7. Read **Genesis 3:1-7**. What happened? First Eve, then Adam, rebelled against God's directive by eating from the tree of knowledge of good and evil. She was enticed by Satan's words, which contained some truth mixed with a lie, but rather than turning to her husband for counsel on whether to eat the fruit or not, she alone made the decision to eat and sin. This effectively removed Eve from the protection of her husband as head of the family—God's design for marriage. Adam then ate of the fruit, deliberately choosing to sin. God always holds the husband responsible!

8. We call this event **the fall**. Read **Genesis 3:14-19**. What was the result of *the fall*? *The result was God's curse:* the serpent would crawl on its belly (vv 14) and there would be hostility between the serpent and his children and the woman and her children **(vv 15)**; *women* would have great pain during childbirth, *would desire to dominate their husbands, but men would rule their wives,* **(vv 16)**; men would have to work hard to make a living **(vv 17-19a)**; finally, death would result for all **(vv 19b)**.

Clearly, the curse dramatically affected marriage: "*And you will desire* **to control your husband,** *but* **he will rule over you**." **[Genesis 3:16b]** Ever hear the phrase, *the war between the sexes*? Here was the battle's beginning, with the effects of God's curse causing contention between husband and wife: women no longer would desire to be submissive, choosing to let their husbands lead, but to dominate and have *headship* (leadership) in the family; husbands, rather than leading the family with godly wisdom, kindness and compassion, would either not assume that role and/or would harshly abuse their authority to maintain control over their wives.

Young women, how will you choose to face the issues of *helper, headship,* and *submission* in today's society? With the feminist agenda and movement so strong in America, these terms are not often deemed acceptable for a wife. Let's examine them more closely for a moment.

Do you possibly misunderstand *headship*, thinking it means your future husband would hold a more important position or be more valuable than you in the family? What about *submission*, when, *in trust*, you would ***voluntarily*** allow your husband to have leadership in your family? Would this make him a *harsh, dictatorial head*, and would submitting require you to acquiesce to his every desire, making you your husband's doormat? You might ask yourself, "*Will home be a safe place?*"

How are you to deal with these thoughts as compared with God's perfect design for marriage and the effects of the *curse*? It is important you remember that when you accepted Christ as your Savior, you became a new creation **(2 Corinthians 5:17)** and that the Holy Spirit came to dwell in you to give you strength to follow God's design with an obedient, loving, and devoted heart **(Acts 2:38-39)**. You are then able to resist what the world tells you regarding marriage and live with faith in the One who is always trustworthy, desiring the best for you and a future family.

If, in spite of this, you still struggle with the idea of becoming a submissive helper to your future husband and not being equal in the role of *heading* your family, think on God Himself...the Holy Trinity...Father, Son, and Holy Spirit, three in One—our best and perfect example of *headship, submission,* and *love.*

Are any members of the Trinity less important or less valuable than the others? ***<u>Absolutely not! All are equally God!</u>*** Even so, do the members of the Trinity maintain certain distinct roles? Is there a *headship*, and do any of the three practice *submission*?

9. Read **Matthew 3:17** and **Luke 3:22**. What does God call Jesus? His Son.

10. Read **John 5:18**. What does Jesus call God? His Father.

11. Now read **Matthew 26:36-39**. Jesus says, "*not as I will, but as You will.*" What is Jesus doing? He is submitting His will to His Father's.

12. Is there a headship in the Trinity? If so, who is the head? Yes, God the Father is head.

13. Is there submission in the Trinity? If so, who submits? Yes, Jesus submits Himself to His Father's will as does the Spirit.

So, in the Trinity, the Father does have *headship*. Jesus, God Himself, equal to God the Father and the Holy Spirit, identifies Himself as the ***Son of God*** and places Himself under the authority of the One whom He calls ***FATHER***. Christ not only prayed regularly to His ***Father*** for guidance, but in Jesus' most anguished moments in the Garden of Gethsemane, He ***willingly*** and ***humbly submitted*** His will to His Father in obedience, "*Yet I want **Your will** to be done, **not Mine**.*"

So what about the Holy Spirit? Read the following passages: **John 14:17, John 14.26**, and **John 16:4**.

14. What do these verses tell you? The Holy Spirit's role in the Trinity is ***Helper***. He teaches believers all truths about Jesus; He helps us understand who God is, the depth of His love, and the importance of obeying Him. He gives His children guidance, wisdom, strength, and boldness. Leaders, give examples of the

disciples' actions before and after Pentecost!

In the Trinity, then, the Holy Spirit is Helper…our glorious helper! He *submits* by not voicing separate thoughts from the Father and Son, but speaks what He has heard, bringing us God's wisdom to guide and strengthen us so that our lives will glorify Christ.**(John 16:13)**

One God, three persons…Father, Son, and Spirit…all with distinctly different roles, but all ***EQUALLY GOD***—this is the mystery of the Holy Trinity, the great ***"I AM…"* [Exodus 3:14]** *This is **PERFECTION!***

Hopefully, after this peek at the Trinity, you better understand the importance of the roles of *headship*, *helper*, and *submission* and why it is so important for us to imitate God's perfect example. By remaining true to God's design for men and women, a marriage will flourish and that union will function, as some would say, like a *well-oiled* machine!

Marriage—two people…husband and wife…equal spiritually and intellectually because both are made in God's image.

1 Peter 3:7b: *"She is your equal partner in God's gift of new life."*

Galatians 3:28 *"There is no longer Jew or Gentile, slave or free, male and female. For you are all one in Christ Jesus."*

Young women…when you marry, you will be your husband's equal, but you *do* have a different role to maintain in the family to complement and strengthen him. God has given you a ***unique*** and ***awesome physiological*** design which will allow you to bear children if you choose to marry. You also have ***fabulous minds***, and with greater connections between the left and right hemispheres in your brain, you can offer insight into situations your future husbands might not see. Then, when you do offer in love your opinions on issues,

which as your husband's helper you need to do, expressing and/or clarifying your ideas and concerns, your husband will be better able make well-informed final decisions for the current and future welfare of your entire family. This does *not* mean your husband will make every decision in your family, for a husband after God's heart will understand your strengths and talents, leaving certain decisions and responsibilities in your family to you, e.g. budgeting and paying

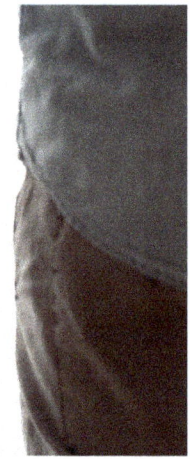

bills if you are disciplined and better with numbers; but ultimately, God will hold your husband responsible for well-being of your family.

What a *privilege* it will be to become your husband's *helper* should you marry. Picture yourself with a heart like Jesus'—a humble, servant's heart. With the Holy Spirit strengthening you, you will become your mate's greatest human helper, strengthening him; and with the perfect ***Helper*** whom Christ sent—the Holy Spirit—further strengthening him, your husband will become the family leader God wants him to be. Then burdens will be removed from your back onto his, and you will experience great freedom and joy. Your entire family will benefit from your example and his, and your loving and obedient heart will be a sweet fragrance to the Lord.

Young men, your physiology specifically equips you to be the provider, defender, and head of a future family. Fantastic, right?! However, after reading what God asks of you in **Ephesians 5:25-30**, can you even begin to imagine the responsibilities He is placing on you? As *head* of the family, you are to love your wives as Jesus loved His church, and that love was all-encompassing! You, therefore, will be responsible and accountable for that same all-encompassing love regarding your wife and family.

Think about Jesus and how He devoted His all to the church. He was her great spiritual teacher who lived what He taught, teaching the meaning of grace, mercy, love, and compassion, while readily pointing out hypocrisy and sin.

As a future husband, you will be the spiritual leader of your family. You can lead your wife by taking her to church and reading Scripture with her, but equally and possibly more important is for you to become a living example of Scripture! To do this, you will need to be in God's Word constantly, seeking the wisdom of the Holy Spirit to understand how deeply Jesus loved His church and what He was willing to give up for her; once understood, you will need to practice these things. Equally important is that you lead your life

in submission to God the Father, just as Jesus did; this example of obedient submission helps you become a credible *head of the family*.

Following are just a few verses demonstrating Jesus' heart toward His church, a heart which you are to imitate in your relationship with your wife-to-be. Read these passages, then explain your responsibilities as a husband. Your answers will be followed by my thoughts.

15. **Matthew 20:28** *"For even the Son of Man came not to be served but to serve others and to give His life as a ransom for many."* _____

_____
_____
_____
_____
_____
_____
_____

You are to serve your wife, thinking of her and her needs as first and foremost in your life. Jesus, though King, had a servant's heart! Desiring the best for His people, He guided believers with humbleness, kindness, and gentleness. Your family will be your kingdom, yet you are not to behave as a hardened, harsh dictator, but with a tender heart like Jesus, guide your wife in a kind, gentle, and humble manner. She will be your queen—your cherished helper and partner—one to be treasured, never serving as your slave or doormat.

16. Jesus is our *"great high priest."* **[Hebrews 4:14]** and *"... Christ Jesus died for us and was raised to life for us, and he is sitting in the place of honor at God's right hand, **pleading for us**."* **[Romans 8:34]**

_____
_____
_____
_____
_____
_____
_____
_____

As Christ continually prays for believers and intercedes to His Father for us, you must pray and intercede for your wife. Desiring her welfare and that she be made *holy, clean*, and *spotless* before God, you will pray for her daily. You also will pray for wisdom and guidance for yourself, as Jesus prayed to

His father, so that your words and actions toward your wife will not be harsh but demonstrate those of Christ's love for His church.

17. *"In the same way, husbands ought to love their wives as they love their own bodies. For a man who loves his wife actually shows love for himself."* **[Eph. 5:28]** _____

_____

_____

_____

It is a rare case when a man does not treat himself with care, respect, and love, desiring the best for himself!

18. *"But God showed his great love for us by sending Christ to die for us while we were still sinners."* **[Romans 5"8]** _____

_____

_____

_____

_____

_____

_____

_____

_____

_____

Just as Jesus did, you must love your wife at all times, even if she is *out of sorts* or *contrary* (which she will be, from time to time—those female hormones do act up!), and even if she *sins against you* in

some manner. As Jesus did, you need to be forgiving and willing to *give your all* for your wife. This is agape love—this is God's heart!

19. *"We know what real love is because Jesus gave up his life for us. So we also ought to give up our lives for our brothers and sisters."* **[1 John 3:16]** _____

_____
_____
_____
_____
_____
_____
_____

As a husband, you ***do*** need to lay down your life for your wife. It is true that this looks different than being crucified on a cross, but it does mean daily living for Christ, crucifying and removing from your life anything that is not of God and replacing it with righteous living and example. It means dying to selfishness and living for her… and not just once or when you are in the mood, but always.

A husband placing his wife's needs first in his life.

These are just a few verses demonstrating Jesus' love for the church, but let's also look at how Christ treated women. In a culture that did not exalt women, He did! Just look at how He treated Mary, Martha, Mary Magdalene, the woman at the well, the adulterous woman, the woman with hemorrhoids, and Mary, His own mother. Jesus had high regard for women, blessed them, and treated them well! In this, He exemplified His Father, who also provided for and blessed women who were treated unfairly: Leah with Jacob, Sarah with Abimelech, Hagar with Abraham, Tamar with Judah, Rahab, etc. These examples provide great lessons for respecting and caring for wives. Leaders—you may want to discuss these.

Once more, how are you, as a future husband, to treat your wife? You are to treat her as Jesus treated His church. As I think on Him, pictures become etched in my: Christ, enduring insults, slander, torture, and death, yet giving His all because of His love for us, wanting no person to perish but have everlasting life. Now that's love, and such is the self-sacrificing responsibility given to husbands.

A final question for you: Do you, as a future wife *or* you, as a future husband, love God enough to trust Him with His design for marriage and act in humble obedience to that with wife as submissive helper and husband as head of the family? This is a heart question and issue, one which you need to ask yourself and answer in truth before marriage.

DO I

TRUST

GOD'S

PLAN ? ?

*When a husband treats his wife
as Christ
treated His church . . .*

*SHE is validated
and knows she is
loved as Christ loved . . .*

Personal Time – Week Five – Day One

This week, during Personal Time, I will be asking you to examine the marriage relationships in your sphere: your parents, guardians, relatives, parents of friends, etc. Be honest about what you see and don't see. I'll be honest about mine, and so will Terry about his. During today's personal time, after reading our stories, I would like you to write about what you see in the marriage of your parents or guardians.

Candice's Story: In looking back on my parents, who were married for sixty-three years, I wonder what formed their personalities and their relationship to one another. My father's parents were married for about that same period of time, with my grandfather being devoted to my grandmother, even seeing her through her many years of Alzheimer's. My mother's parents, on the other hand, were divorced when she was twenty-three. Those were the days when divorce was very much frowned upon, and it required a trial. My mother had to go to court, testifying that her mom was an adulteress, which I believe scarred my mom for life. Perhaps that's why she stayed with my father those many years, in spite of confessing to me on her fiftieth wedding anniversary she would have left Dad if he had more money. This confession broke my heart!

When I was small, I do remember happy times. Mom and Dad seemed to enjoy one another—golfing, playing bridge with friends, and dressing up for evening parties in our basement; guests would drink at Dad's bar and dance to the big bands of the 1950s. I can still hear Tommy Dorsey, Duke Ellington, and Stan Kenton's

music playing on vinyl records. Although the noise grew quite loud for little ears, I loved sneaking down the stairs and watching Mom and Dad glide around the room, waltzing with grace and ease. These were their good times, yet as years passed, an overriding darkness prevailed, and I wrote many poems about the distress I felt during my teenage years feeling my mom and dad would divorce.

When I think on Mom and Dad's marriage, I think of bitter years of fighting, cursing, and screaming. Often when upset, my

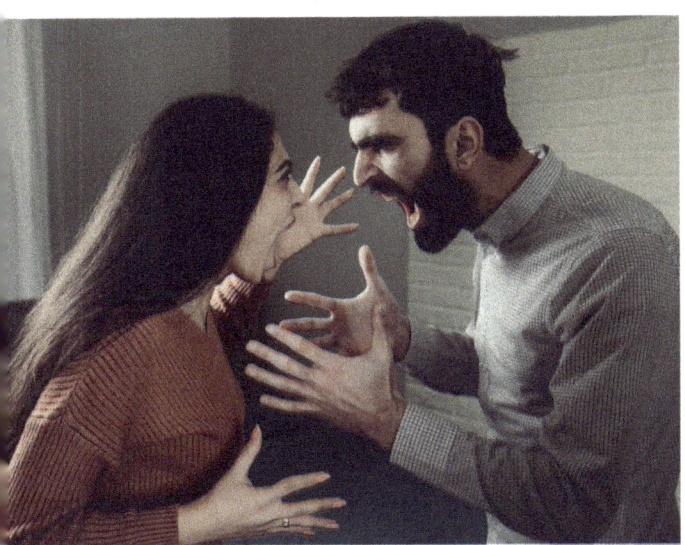

mom would leave the house and, several times, left for days without letting any of us know where she had gone or when she would be back. At other times, Mom would withdraw, not speaking to us, and this silence sometimes lasted for weeks. It seemed, at times, there was no pleasing her, so during my high school years, my dad often took me to the golf course after he got off work to remove us both from Mom's emotional outbursts.

In contrast to my mom and dad, God gave me a beautiful example of a loving relationship in marriage when, in the sixth grade, He brought a new friend into my life. Karen and I became very close, and I spent much time at her home. Karen's parents were years younger and much poorer than mine, but that didn't seem to matter to them; what I do remember is an overwhelming sense of calm, peace, and joy in their home. This family gathered together every Sunday afternoon at one of the grandparents' homes for family dinners, and I remember longing for that type of family closeness. Also, there is one vivid picture that remains clear in my mind to this very day, and that is of Karen's mom and dad squeezing into a chair together in their basement, laughing, tickling each other, kissing, then blushing when they saw we were watching. I didn't know such a relationship could exist!

While my parents were fighting over any and every little thing, especially money, this couple laughed and loved and treated their children with respect and care. This set an example for me of a strong, healthy relationship between husband and wife.

I do want you to know that, in spite of everything I've written, God gave me proof of an underlying love between Mom and Dad, hidden in the sands beneath tumultuous waters. Terry had picked up my mother, who as my grandmother had dementia, to take her to my dad's bedside as he was dying. In a moment of clarity, Mom leaned toward Dad and said, "I love you," to which he replied, "I love you, too, Sweetheart." This sweet sentiment and truth still brings tears to my eyes, and it will always be one of my fondest memories.

Thank you, LORD, for allowing me to witness the battles that can rage in a marriage so that I could understand, in contrast, a strong, beautiful relationship between husband and wife. Karen's parents beautifully exemplified what marriage could be and became a model of the one I would eventually have with Terry!

Terry's story: As far back as I can remember, my parents had a dysfunctional marriage. As a young child, I can remember being in

the very back of our Ford station wagon and hearing my parents fighting. Mom got out of the car and slammed the door as my older brother and I were crying in the back seat. My dad asked my brother what to do, and he said, "Go get her!"

At some point in those very early years (I was in either kindergarten or first grade), the pressure on my mom mounted and

she had a breakdown (which we never talked about). I was sent to live with my mom's parents in McMinnville, Oregon, while my brother was sent to my dad's parents in Compton, California. I spent the rest of the school year in McMinnville and was there at least six months as I have pictures of me at Christmas and in the spring there.

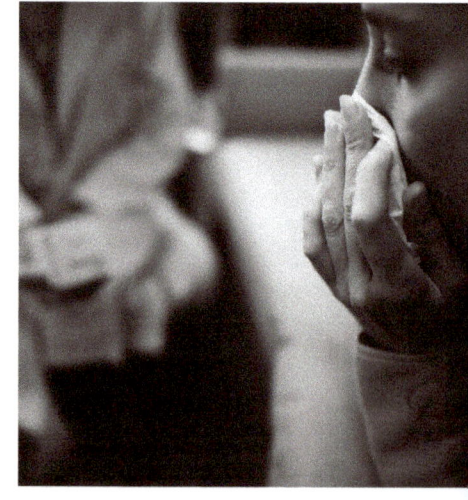

In late 1957 my Dad was involved in a horrible motorcycle

accident, when he (a LAPD motorcycle policeman) was purposely rammed into by a man driving approximately fifty miles an hour; Dad had earlier cited this man with a traffic violation. Dad flew through the air about 150 feet, had many broken bones, part of his head damaged so that he went deaf in one ear, and had to learn to walk all over again. This must have put a great strain on Mom and her marriage, trying to raise an eighth grader, fourth grader, and a two-year old all by herself.

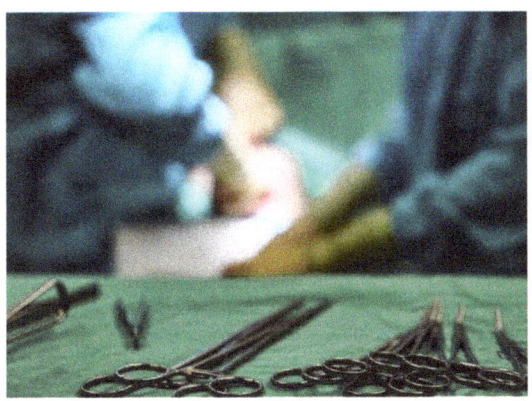

This is when Mom and Dad sold their house in California and moved to Tenmile. That was *home* from 1960-1978 until my parents divorced (for the first time). During the years I was home, Dad was very angry at almost everything. He had lost a career he loved and was not the man physically he had been just a few years before. I am sure now, looking back, that this also added to the tension between Mom and Dad. They used very unkind language toward each other (more so my dad than mom), and the use of foul words was common.

As I related earlier, my parents

did not have any relationship with Christ or attend church, even after Grandma Zelma and I started to go. I invited Pastor Black to come out to the house and talk to Dad about going to church, but Dad was against this. He had become a Mason sometime earlier, and that became his *church* and belief system, rather than Christ.

When I was twenty-nine, my parents were divorced and sold the farm. Funny thing, they got back together and remarried for a year, then realized why they had divorced in the first place and got divorced again! Mom ended up remarrying, but this man who also turned out to have a bad temper, died within several years of the marriage. Dad moved to Arizona and spent his last years living with a woman.

Thinking about the marriages of my mom and dad, I realize that having Jesus as the focal point of the union and building on the foundation of God's truths makes all the difference in keeping the marriage covenant and of not only having peace in the marriage, but having joy. You may ask how things ended for Mom and Dad. I'm

God's TRUTHS must become our foundation in the covenant of marriage.

delighted to tell you that Candice and I were able to take Mom to a non-denominational service where Mom responded to an altar call to receive the Lord as her Savior. Hallelujah! We will see her again! I'm not certain about Dad's salvation, though. I only saw him two times from 1978 until 1996, that second time when my sister called me from Las Vegas, Nevada, where Dad had been admitted to the hospital. I flew down and sat with him during his last two days. He never once said he loved me, that he was sorry about anything he had done, or that he had any hope of being with Jesus after he passed. To the very end, he was stubborn, closed off, and unforgiving of others. This breaks my heart! *"Jesus…Dad needed You! I hope he reached for you in his last moments and that we will see him again!"*

Your story: _____

_____
_____
_____
_____
_____
_____
_____
_____
_____
_____
_____
_____

Now pray and ask God, "Are *YOU* the focus of my family's life?" Write how that 'yes' or 'no' has affected your story.

_____
_____
_____
_____
_____
_____
_____
_____
_____
_____
_____
_____

Jesus, please ALWAYS
the focus of my future family!

Personal Time – Week Five – Day Two

Although you have discussed **Eph 5:21-25** as a group, take time now to write how these verses apply to you personally. What do they have to do with your heart, and how do you see these playing out in your role as a future husband or wife?

"And further, submit to one another out of reverence for Christ. For wives, this means submit to your husbands as to the Lord. For a husband is the head of his wife as Christ is the head of the church. He is the Savior of His body, the church. As the church submits to Christ, so you wives should submit to your husbands in everything. For husbands, this means love your wives, just as Christ loved the church. He gave us His life for her." _____

Personal Time – Week Five – Day Three

Review **1 Cor. 13:4-8** and **Eph. 4:2**.

Eph. 4:32 *"Instead, be kind to each other, tenderhearted, forgiving one another, just as God through Christ has forgiven you."*

1 Cor. 13:4-8 *"Love is patient and kind. Love is not jealous or boastful or proud or rude. It does not demand its own way. It is not irritable, and it keeps no record of being wronged. It does not rejoice about injustice but rejoices whenever the truth wins out. Love never gives up, never loses faith, is always hopeful, and endures through every circumstance."*

Spend a few minutes in prayer, then examine your heart carefully to see how you *measure up* to what God is teaching you about love...***His kind of love***. Are you kind and tenderhearted? Do you forgive or hold grudges, counting the wrongs others have done to you? Are you jealous of others, boastful, demanding to get your own way? Are you proud, rude, irritable? Do you **stand tall** when situations get difficult, remaining hopeful and enduring through tough times, or do you easily get depressed, losing faith in others?

Write what God reveals to you on the next page, noting the ways you do and don't demonstrate His *compassionate* love. Are there areas in which you can improve on **standing tall** and being Christ's image bearer? Explain.

How Tall Do I Stand *Compared to 1 Corinthians 13:4-8?*

Personal Time – Week Five – Day Four

God has revealed through His Word His design for marriage. Based on what you have studied in Scripture and spending time with the Lord in prayer, have you formed any new convictions about marriage, your heart, and/or what love should be to create a successful union? If so, write these down and any *unshakable unbreakables* based on them. _____

_____
_____
_____
_____
_____
_____
_____
_____
_____
_____
_____
_____
_____

A few weeks ago, I was directed to an excellent sermon on marriage. Please check Notes/Sources after Week 5 for more information. You may wish to add an extra week to watch this.

DIGGING IN – WEEK SIX – GROUP TIME

Jesus Stands Tall Regarding Divorce

We've now arrived at that very tough topic—divorce. It's never an easy subject to discuss, but it is one that is necessary. I would like you to keep in mind one thing, however. If you are a committed Christian who took to heart everything studied in Weeks Four and Five (you'll need to go over these principles with a future spouse), the word divorce will **never** become a part of your vocabulary! Zip, zero, nada! No, no one expects you to be perfect now or in marriage, or a spouse for that matter, *"for everyone has sinned; we all fall short of God's glorious standard,"* **[Romans 3:23]** ; but, if you love God with all your heart, soul, mind, and strength and others as yourself; if you accept Jesus as your Savior and grow in Him, attending church regularly, studying God's Word, praying, and surrendering fully to God's Spirit and direction; and if you follow God's creative design of wives being helpers, submitting to their husbands for leadership and of husbands being the heads and leaders of their families, then rather than drifting apart in marriage, you will be drawn ever closer together with your spouse in oneness. In spite of differences, each will become the other's greatest champion and strength and the union will be strong. This is the road God wants you to choose—the one that often is *less traveled.*1 If you remain true to the covenant of your marriage and a servant to your mate, vowing to remain faithful at all times, your marriage will be a success.

Still, there are marriages where both bride and groom state they are Christians and attend church, but their stated belief system does not match their life actions. Why? Attending church does not necessarily make a strong commitment to the Lord. God's Word may be heard, even read, but not acted upon. You may accept Christ as Savior in an emotional moment, but never grow in Him. What happens then, when you do not **long** for God *"As a deer pants for flowing streams, so pants my soul for you, O God. My soul thirsts for God, for the living God."*? **[Psalm 42:1-2 ESV]** What happens when you do not desire a heart change, one that becomes more like Christ? It's like placing a cork in a bottle of choice wine; nothing you desire will come out! You will struggle to overcome the lust of the world and will lack the desire to become obedient to God's design for your life and a possible future marriage.

So what happens in a marriage that is unequally yoked, with one being a believer and the other not? What happens when two non-believers marry? What happens when a tragedy in the family occurs, such as the death of a child? While these marriages may survive the surging floodwaters of trials and temptations, you can be assured that without Christ it will be hard, if not impossible, and many times the ending of your story will not be the happy one of Cinderella and Prince Charming riding off into the sunset to live happily ever after.

Let's look at current statistics that validate what we've studied so far. Research from 1972 through the late 2010's does give evidence that **being a committed Christian does affect the longevity of marriage.** Brian J. Hollar, Associate Professor of Economics at Marymount University in Arlington, VA, writes, "Many pastors and pundits claim that divorce rates between Christians and non-Christians are the same. But this statistic is misleading at best and grossly understates the actual connection between religion and marriage. For nearly 50 years, people who attend church regularly marry at much higher rates and, for a majority of the population, those who attend church frequently also divorce at lower rates than the rest of the population." [2]

Study the following bar graphs from this article, then as a group, talk about and write down your conclusions. (Note: In this study, those who were considered devout Christians attended church three or more times a month compared to non-devout attending once or less; men and women were of ages twenty-five through fifty-four; and because the study was started in 1972, the only demographics were white, black, and other.)

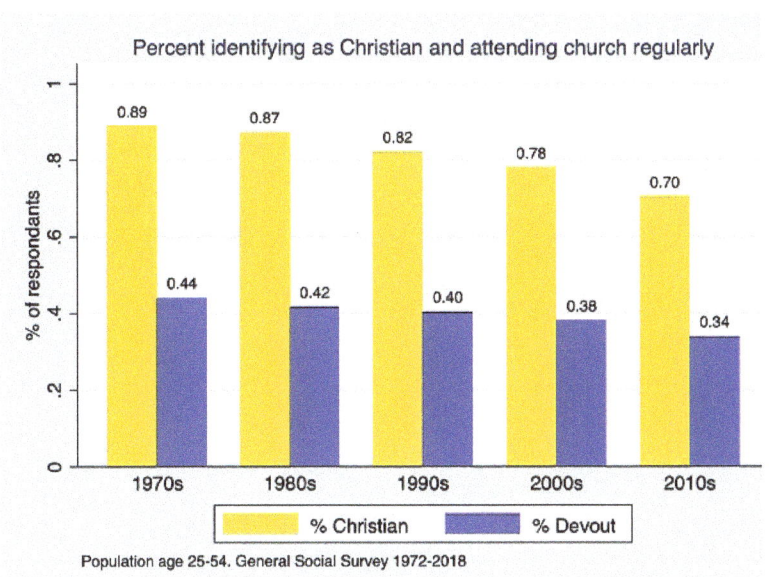

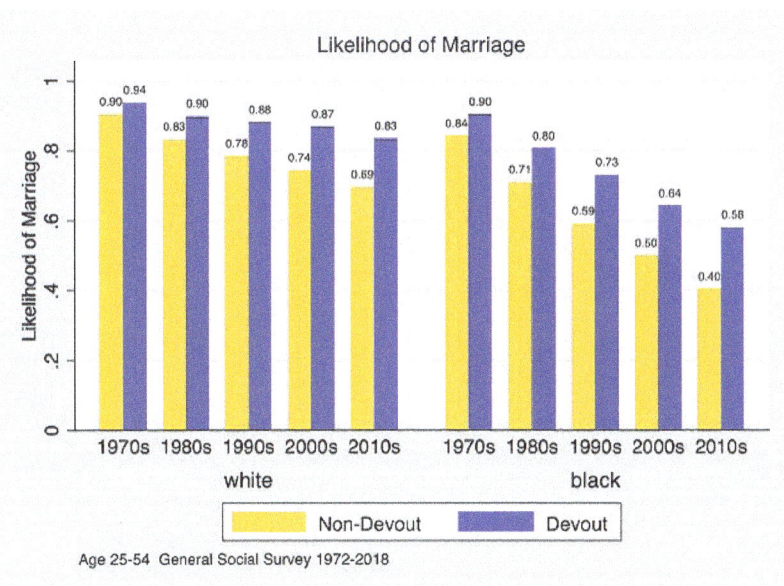

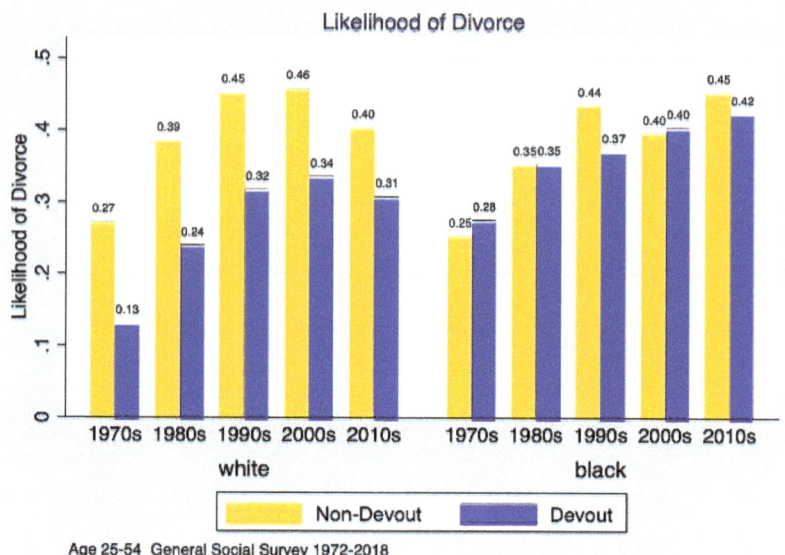

Age 25-54 General Social Survey 1972-2018

1. Do those who are not devoted followers of Christ identify themselves as Christians? Yes

2. Are devout Christians more likely to marry than those who are not? Yes

3. Are devout Christians less likely to divorce than non-Christians? Yes   Has the difference between the two groups dropped over the years? Yes

4. Between 1972 and now, has the attendance of Christians at church risen or declined? Declined.   Non-devout Christians? Declined.   Devout Christians? Declined

5. Between 1972 and now, has the likelihood of marriage risen or declined? Declined.   Explain why you think this has happened? During the past century, God, prayers, and the Ten

Commandments have been removed from schools, and the Bible is no longer the basis for school learning as it was in the early 1800's. Christian faith is now being challenged in the political arena, and living together is deemed acceptable, etc. All this is summed up by statistics that demonstrate that as church attendance declined, so did the rate of marriage for Christians, both devout (36% drop) and non-devout (50%). This indicates that a strong relationship with Christ and obedience to God's commands is essential to believing in the institution of marriage, and that being a member of a church body that encourages and teaches this is tantamount.

6. Why do you think devout Christians are less likely to divorce than non-devout?   Devout Christians are committed to living as Christ did, self-sacrificially and as a servant to their spouses and others.

7. Do you think the marriage/divorce statistics would differ even more if there was one more category included in the research for committed, growing Christians—those who read their Bibles daily, acted upon what God's Word said, and prayed? Yes   Explain. As we spend time in God's Word, praying to Him and listening for His voice, we are being sanctified—becoming more like Him. The more we are like Christ, the more we are willing to love our spouse with an agape love—one that is unconditional—one that is willing to sacrifice for our mate.

Let's get back to what God says in His Word about divorce, noting that in Old Testament times, only husbands could seek and file certificates of divorce. Read aloud **Deuteronomy 6:4-5** and

Leviticus 19:18. Select teens to read aloud.

8. **In Deuteronomy 6:4-5**, what commandment corresponds to what Jesus taught? *"Listen, O Israel! The Lord is our God, the Lord alone. And you must love the Lord your God with all your heart, all your soul, and all your strength"* corresponds with Matthew 22:37. Jesus quotes this as the first and greatest commandment.

9. What is the commandment given in **Leviticus 19:18**? *"Do not seek revenge or bear a grudge against a fellow Israelite, but love your neighbor as yourself. I am the Lord,"* which corresponds to Jesus' statement of the second greatest commandment in Matthew 22:38.

Now read **Malachi 2: 10-11**:

¹⁰*"Are we not all children of the same Father? Are we not all created by the same God? Then why do we **betray each other**, violating the covenant of our ancestors? ¹¹ Judah has been unfaithful, and a detestable thing has been done in Israel and in Jerusalem. The men of Judah have **defiled the Lord's beloved sanctuary** by marrying women who worship idols.* 12

May the Lord cut off from the nation of Israel every last man who has done this and yet brigs an offering to the LORD of Heaven's Armies." NLT

Other Bible versions of *betray each other* translate the phrase to say *treat each other treacherously* (HCS) or *are faithless to one another* (ESV).

10. Based on verse 10, how are the children of Israel treating each other? Treacherously, by betrayal. They certainly are not obeying God's commandment to love one another as themselves.

11. As defined by verse 11, how have the Israelites profaned the LORD's sanctuary? They have married women from other nations. These non-Jewish women were bound to have a profoundly negative effect on husbands and children, bringing into the home the worship of false gods and idols, leading families spiritually astray and away from the one true God.

In both betraying their brethren and by marrying outside the Israelite nation, Jewish men were doing something detestable to God, and this defiled His sanctuary. Equally detestable to God was the treacherous betrayal of wedding vows, as often a divorce from an Israelite wife was required before marrying a woman from another nation. Read aloud several different versions of **Malachi 2:13-16** to learn God's reaction. Teens read several versions aloud.

A woman is being divorced by her husband so he may marry someone he considers prettier.

12. In verse 16, how do your versions differ? Some translate as *"God hates divorce!"* (NLT, NASB, NKJ, etc.) while others translate *"If he (the husband) hates and divorces his wife," says the Lord God of Israel, "he covers his garment with injustice..."* (CSB, ESV, NIV, HCS, etc.)

The variances in wording arise because of differing interpretations in Hebrew grammar, some translating in the first person, *I*, meaning God; some translating in the third person, meaning *he*, the husband. However, one thing stands clear: betraying wedding vows was not God's plan.

13. Based on all versions of Malachi, what was a result of a man's being unfaithful to his wife? Offerings and prayers made to the Lord were not acceptable because of unfaithfulness.

14. What did God desire in marriage? He desired Jewish men to be faithful to the wives they first married, never breaking their vows to care for them.

15. What was God's heart for children? He desired godly children.

Read **Deuteronomy 6:1-9**.

16. How were children to be raised to become godly? In the book of Exodus, parents were commanded to teach their children what God had done to establish and save the Israelite nation. In Deuteronomy, they were instructed to *"repeat God's commands again and again, at home, on the road, when going to bed and when getting up."* Parents were to tie the commands to their hands and wear them on their foreheads; they were to be written on the doorposts of their homes and on their gates. What a reminder for children!

17. Why do you think that God said that to divorce a wife is "to overwhelm her with cruelty"? **[Malachi 2:16]** Ideas: When a man divorced his wife, he removed the protection he was to provide for her.

God protects us as an umbrella from rain when we stay under His authority. So also should a husband protect his wife.

A footnote from the Holman ChristianStandard Study Bible states: "Their husbands were 'hating' so as to 'divorce' them for no legitimate reason **[Deuteronomy 24:3]**, which was a heinous injustice. Such a cold-blooded and unscrupulous traitor to his marital responsibilities who would deny his wife the very things he had pledged to provide—devotion, care, companionship, protection, intimacy, peace, justice **[Gn 2:2; Ex 21:10; Dt 22:13-19; Pr 5:15-20]**— stood condemned by God, and he wore the stain of his crime like a garment for all to see **[Ps 73:6]**." 3

18. Going back to God desiring godly children as a result of marriage, what could happen to children during Old Testament times and today as a result of divorce? In the Old Testament, children would be led astray to worship false gods. Today, they may feel guilt—that their behavior caused the divorce. They may show negative behaviors in a number of ways because they suffer from a lack of time and interaction with either their father or mother. The hurt sometimes requires life-long counseling to deal with their pain and to learn how to lead whole, fulfilling, positive, and relational lives with another. All of these are adverse reactions to divorce, drawing children away from God and from His perfect plan for their lives.

19. Draw some conclusions based on the study of **Malachi 2:10-13.** God was very much opposed to divorce. He was an advocate for women; His design intended that they be loved, cared for, and protected by their husbands.

Let's turn now to the Pharisees when they tested Jesus, questioning Him about divorce. At the time of Jesus, there were two major and conflicting houses (schools) of thought existing: the House of Hillel and the House of Shammai. 4,5 In the matter of divorce, Hillel and Shammai interpreted certain words in Scripture differently, and as in the case of Malachi, this resulted in variant conclusions.

Regarding divorce, both schools turned to **Deuteronomy 24:1-4**:

"When a man takes a wife and marries her, if then she finds no favor in his eyes because he has found some indecency in her, and he writes her a certificate of divorce and puts it in her hand and sends her out of his house, and she departs out of his house, ² and if she goes and becomes another man's wife, ³ and the latter man hates her and writes her a certificate of divorce and puts it in her hand and sends her out of his house, or if the latter man dies, who took her to be his wife, ⁴ then her former husband, who sent her away, may not take her again to be his wife, after she has been defiled, for that is an abomination before the LORD. And you shall not bring sin upon the land that the LORD your God is giving you for an inheritance."

Notice that verses one through three use **if** statements. This means that these are conditional, and only verse four tells what happened based upon those conditions: if a man married, divorced that woman to marry another, he may not divorce that second wife to go back and remarry his first wife. (Some Israelite men would do this repeatedly! UGH!) Nevertheless, the schools of Hillel and Shammai focused especially on verse one as giving reason for divorce: *"When a man takes a wife and marries her, if then she finds no favor in his* *eyes because **he has found some indecency** in her…*" (ESV, NASB) The emphasis for Shammaites was on **some indecency in her**, meaning **unfaithfulness to the husband**; for the Hillelites, the emphasis was on **something**, the word itself, which resulted in **for any reason**… **HUGE DIFFERENCE!** For us today, the grammatical difference would be something like interpreting "Would you like to eat Sarah?" versus "Would you like to eat, Sarah?" Sarah would freak out at the first sentence and jump to the table in the second!

With regard to divorce, then, the Shammai house interpreted Scripture very strictly while Hillel's did very liberally, with divorce being based on outrageous excuses such as a wife burning food or finding another woman more attractive. Wives, watch out for those bushy eyebrows, pale cheeks, and charred steaks!

With this in mind, again consider the Pharisees' words in their attempt to ambush Jesus, *"Should a man be allowed to divorce his wife for just any reason?"* desiring Him to choose one house of thought over the OTHER. **[Matthew 19:3]**

" *'Haven't you read the Scriptures?' Jesus replied. 'They record that from the beginning God made them male and female. And He said, 'This explains why a man leaves his father and mother and is joined to his wife, and the two are united into one.' Since they are no longer two but one,* **let no one split apart what God has joined together.***' "* [Matthew 19:4-6]

Of course Jesus knew the Pharisees read the Scriptures; they were the teachers of God's Word to the Jewish nation! They devoted themselves to study and believed in strictly following all written and oral laws of Judaism as well as its traditions. 6

Jesus' words taunted the Pharisees as He reviewed with them God's truths:

- God created humans male and female.

- God joined man and woman together as one.

- God <u>commanded</u>, *"let no one split apart what God has joined together."* (The words **let** is a command; it is not a suggestion.)

The Pharisees definitely took offense at this, but they continued to question Jesus: *"Why then did Moses **command** one to give a certificate of divorce and to send her away?"* **[Matthew 19:7 ESV, NASB, KJV, NKJV, NIV]** Jesus corrects the devious Pharisees' wording when He responds, *"Moses **permitted** divorce only as a concession to your hard hearts, **but it was not what God had originally intended.** And I tell you this, whoever divorces his wife and marries someone else commits adultery—unless his wife has been unfaithful."* **[Matthew 19: 9]**

Cunning Pharisees—using **command** instead of **permit**, taking what Moses said completely out of context! (Doesn't that remind you of a certain crafty serpent in the Garden of Eden?!) Moses never **commanded** divorce, rather only **permitted** it.

Ultimately, how did Jesus **stand tall** against the assault and persecution of the Pharisees? **Read carefully**: <u>**Never once**</u> did Jesus turn to man for an answer or rebuttal; <u>**never once**</u> did He turn to Hillel or Shammai. No, Jesus *ALWAYS* turned to His Father's Word

for the truth, and this truth was that **marriage is a covenant designed to last a lifetime,** with each spouse committed to the welfare of the other, the husband caring for his wife as Jesus did His church, and the wife being her husband's helper, supporting him through her submission, allowing him to be the head of the family. This was God's truth.

Marriage and divorce, topics so important and vital to your future, they must not be taken lightly. Before considering marriage then, examine yourself. Are you *healthy*, and is the person you are marrying *healthy*? (See pp. 80-90.) Are you a committed Christian who is growing in Christ, and will you be equally yoked to another committed Christian who is also growing in Christ? Finally, are you spiritually strong enough in Christ to fulfill the vows you one day will make in marriage? Will you **stand tall for better or for worse, in sickness and in health, until death do you part?** This is God's recipe for success!

BE HEALTHY

GROW IN CHRIST

MARRY A BELIEVER

STAND TALL IN YOUR COVENANT OF MARRIAGE!

Personal Time – Week Six – Day One

As was taught earlier, marriage is a covenant, and because Almighty God is the author of covenant, it is as unchangeable as His character. In the Old Testament, covenants were sealed by a blood sacrifice, which meant that each party involved in the covenant committed to being killed if he/she broke that covenant. Very serious business, a covenant…and very serious business, **standing tall in marriage**—<u>*remaining true to your covenant*</u>. But if you are a devout believer, you will have the *Holy Spirit—God's Helper*—living within

you, empowering you with God's grace and strength to keep **standing tall** in your marriage. (Note: Now you can better understand why an adulteress was to be stoned in Old Testament law!)

Jesus taught accordingly that the covenant of marriage was unbreakable and that divorce was not what God intended; the only reason Jesus allowed for divorce was a wife's immorality (remember that in Jesus' day only men were allowed to file for divorce; today this would apply to husbands and wives). The Greek word Jesus chose to use for *immorality* was *porneia* meaning **illicit sexual intercourse** which included **adultery, fornication, homosexuality, lesbianism, intercourse with animals, close relatives, or a divorced man or woman.** Jesus did not use the word *moicheia*, which specifically referred to adultery alone.7 Now look up the following: **Matthew 5:31-32; Mark 10:2-12; Luke 16:18.**

1. What do Jesus' disciples teach about divorce? Just like Jesus, they taught that divorce was to be permitted only in the case of immorality.

Read **1 Corinthians 7:39; Romans 7:2-3**.

2. When was a woman allowed to remarry? When her husband died

Read **1 Corinthians 7:12-16**: *"Now, I will speak to the rest of you, though I do not have a direct command from the Lord. If a fellow believer has a wife who is not a believer and she is willing to continue living with him, he must not leave her. And if a believing woman has a husband who is not a believer and he is willing to continue living with her, she must not leave him. For the believing wife brings holiness to her marriage, and the believing husband brings holiness to his marriage. Otherwise, your children would not be holy, but now they are holy. (But if the husband or wife who isn't a believer insists on leaving, let them go. In such cases the believing husband or wife is no longer bound to the other, for God has called you to live in peace. Don't you wives realize that your husbands might be saved because of you? And don't you husbands realize that your wives might be saved because of you?"*

3. Although Paul states that he does not feel his words are a

command from the Lord, what he does say correlates to what God and His Son Jesus have taught. Summarize these verses. When one spouse is a believer and the other is not, marriage should not be dissolved if the unbeliever is willing to stay. This is because the unbeliever may be saved due to the good example of the believer. Only when the unbeliever leaves is the believer free to remarry.

In most versions of the Bible (NIV, ESV, NASB, NKJ, HCS, etc.) Jesus states that divorce *"was not the way in the beginning,"* or as the NLT translates, *"was not what God intended."*

4. Do you think Jesus feels the same about divorce today? Yes Why? Unlike man, God is unchanging. He is truth, and out of that truth He gives commands that, if obeyed, give joy in life. God's command was for husband and wife to stay together throughout life, and there should not be divorce *for just any reason*. Living to serve others—that was Jesus' example, and we are to follow Him in all things. Happy homes, godly children…what could be better?

6. How should you apply what Jesus teaches? Divorce should be the very last resort for a married couple, with reconciliation being the goal.

I will STAND TALL and fight for my marriage!

Yes, God wants us to live according to His standards just as much today as He did in Old Testament times. In marriage, men are to **stand tall**, protecting their wives, treating them as Christ did the church, giving *His ALL* for the salvation of those who would believe in Him; and wives are to **stand tall**, utilizing the many gifts God has given them **(Prov. 31)** to help and complement their husbands.

ON MARRIAGE

"Eve was not taken out of Adam's head to top him, neither out of his feet to be trampled on by him, but out of his side to be equal with him, under his arm to be protected by him, and near his heart to be loved by him." Matthew Henry--1700's

Couples Who've Remained True to their Covenant

Personal Time Personal Time – Week Six – Day Two

We have spent much time looking at marriage, learning it is a lifetime covenant, but what about divorce? Sadly, it is a reality.

The divorce rate, as we noted before, is high in America and often occurs *for just any reason*. Here are some of the *just any reasons* I've heard:

- "I thought I could change my spouse once we were married.
- "My spouse has changed and is not the person I married."
- "The romance we once experienced is gone."
- "The feelings of love I once had for my spouse died."
- "There's no excitement in my marriage."
- "I'm simply not happy."
- "I can't endure the criticism/naggings anymore."
- "My spouse has let herself/himself *go*."
- "My spouse never listens to me."
- "We are always arguing."
- *"I got married a lot,"* he once said. *"But in my head, I'm not a marrying guy. When I grew up, nobody lived together. If you fell in love, you got married. And so I married the ones that I loved. But what I loved at 20 is not what I loved at 30, and what I loved at 30 is not what I loved at 40."* Larry King, who was married seven times!

All of these demonstrate a ***heart problem***. In marriage, *"...If you are trying to figure out the grounds for divorce so that you can get your relationship to qualify, then you have a heart problem."* 9

2. Thinking on these things, what do you think God's main point about marriage and divorce is? Marriage should be entered into with the understanding that it is a lifelong covenant; God stresses keeping marriage vows, for better or worse, and not divorcing. The above are not excuses for divorce; they are reasons for counseling to work through issues.

3. Is there ever a time, however, when a married couple should separate or a divorce be sought? Think about what should happen when a spouse abuses his/her mate and is unrepentant. If there is abuse in marriage, with either husband or wife endangering the other or their children physically and/or verbally, causing mental or emotional trauma, separation should immediately occur. Counsel should be sought through pastors and/or professional Christian counselors. Although reconciliation would still be a goal, change of behavior with a repentant heart must be proven, which requires much time before husband and wife are reunited. In the case of an

unrepentant heart and/or unchanged behavior, I would recommend pastoral counsel .

4. Some churches condemn divorce to the extent that divorcees are looked down upon and made to feel guilt and shame. Do you think this is right? No   Why or why not? Jesus pointed out that we should not condemn others when He addressed those attacking the adulteress, "…let the one who has never sinned throw the first stone!" **[John 8:7b]** "All of us have sinned and fall short of the glory of God." **[Romans 3:23]** When we confess our sins, we are forgiven.

4. My question to you is this: **Is divorce the ultimate sin?** _____

_____
_____
_____

Look up **1 John 1:9**.

5. What does it say? *"If we confess our sins to God, He is faithful and just to forgive us our sins and to cleanse us from all wickedness."*

6. Based on this verse, even if divorce was your fault, when you confess that to God, what happens? You are forgiven and your soul is made pure and clean. Christ died for every sin, including divorce.

7. So is divorce the ultimate sin? No What is the ultimate sin? The ultimate sin is rejecting the Lord Jesus Christ as Savior. This is the only case when sin cannot be forgiven.

THE ULTIMATE SIN (SATAN'S PLAN for YOU) IS REJECTING JESUS

Personal Time – Week Six – Day Three

As we have studied, God desires godly children as a result of marriage. Although children of differing temperaments and ages react differently to divorce, the following are some of the negative effects observed in children after divorce [10], especially when parents have not had loud and frequent confrontations in the home before the divorce and work well together after the divorce (why couldn't they act this way when married?). [11]

- Poor performance in academics

- Loss of interest in social activity
- Difficulty adapting to change
- Emotionally sensitive
- Anger/irritability
- Feelings of guilt
- Destructive behavior
- Increase in health problems
- Loss of faith in marriage and family unit
- Rebellion

1. If your parents are divorced, have you experienced any of the above? If so, please identify the areas in which you have been hurt. What do you think you can do to understand your value to God and others? (Please consider seeking help from a Christian counselor!)

If your parents are not divorced, but you have friends whose parents are, have you seen them display any of the negative behaviors listed? If so, how can you support and help your friends? _____

_____
_____
_____
_____
_____
_____
_____

2. Looking to the future, what are your thoughts about how you might raise godly children—to love God with all their hearts, minds, souls, and strength? _____

_____
_____
_____
_____
_____
_____
_____

Personal Time – Week Six – Day Four

Marriage and divorce—most likely these are life choices that are far in your future. However, sex is not. You are being faced with the choice to abstain from sex until marriage, a **standing tall** choice, or partaking in sex now which the world accepts and promotes.

Please read and carefully study this small excerpt on marriage written by C.S. Lewis many years ago in his book *Mere Christianity*. In it, Lewis described our contemporary struggle with human sexuality with the following words:

"The Christian idea of marriage is based on Christ's words that a man and wife are to be regarded as a single organism—for that is what the words "one flesh" would be in modern English. And the Christians believe that when He said this He was not expressing a sentiment but stating a fact-just as one is stating a fact when one says that a lock and its key are one mechanism, or that a violin and a bow are one musical instrument. The inventor of the human machine was telling us that its two halves, the male and the female, were made to be combined together in pairs, not simply on the sexual level, but totally combined. The monstrosity of sexual intercourse outside marriage is that those who indulge in it are trying to isolate one kind of union (the sexual) from all the other kinds of union which was intended to go along with it and make up the

total union. The Christian attitude does not mean that there is anything wrong about sexual pleasure, any more than about the pleasure of eating. It means that you must not isolate that pleasure and try to get it by itself, any more than you ought to try to get the pleasures of taste without swallowing and digesting, by chewing things and spitting them out again..." 12

1. Write your thoughts about what this passage means. Discuss Lewis's point that there is a oneness, a union, a complete joining together and bonding with sex, even though there are two people. That bonding is something that will always remain. A friend of mine actually went to counseling because, although she had been married for years, she kept dreaming about a former lover. The counselor pointed out that she had bonded with that man, and that is why the memory remained. Ask teens if they think this hurt her husband or marriage relationship.

Again, going back to **Genesis 2**, God created Adam and Eve to become one, and being one was designed for marriage. Based on this, Paul wrote: *"Run from anything that stimulates youthful lusts. Instead, pursue righteous living, faithfulness, love, and peace. Enjoy the companionship of those who call on the Lord with pure hearts."* **[2 Timothy 2:22]** and *"Run from sexual sin! No other sin so clearly affects the body as this one does. For sexual immorality is a sin against your own body."* **[1 Cor. 6:18]**

1. Carefully think on these things, and though it's hard to put on paper, write your thoughts on premarital sex: Is this something you are considering, or is this something you'd like to flee? Why or why

not? _____

_____

_____

_____

_____

2.   Is sex something that already has taken place? If so, how do you feel about that? Teens answer here._____

_____

_____

_____

Would you like to start over? Always remember, that is what God is all about! He is the God of second chances and third chances and fourth chances…and on and on and on! He never gives up! His compassions and mercies are new every day! "The faithful love of the LORD never ends! His mercies never cease. Great is his faithfulness; His mercies begin afresh each morning." **[Lamentations 3:22-23]**

Jesus came to *"heal the brokenhearted and bandage their wounds."* **[Psalm 147:3]** *"He came to restore what the locusts have eaten."* **[Joel 2:25]** All it takes is for you to confess that you've sinned and ask God to forgive you and restore your righteousness through Jesus. If you'd like to do this, take a moment right now and confess your sin. You can either do this in your head, out loud, or write below. Then choose **to stand tall** and live a pure life from this day forward. Teens have the option of writing here. _____

_____

After this study, do you have any new convictions and *unshakable*

"Come now, let's settle this," says the Lord. "Though your sins are like scarlet, I will make them as white as snow. Though they are red like crimson, I will make them as white as wool."
Isaiah 1:18

unbreakables regarding marriage, divorce, and/or premarital sex? If so, write your new convictions regarding these topics, and in particular, premarital sex. If you have had premarital sex and have repented, perhaps you can make a list of dating rules for yourself, which become your *unshakable unbreakables*. Here are some I've heard—honestly!

- "I will always double date."
- "If I go on a single date, I won't allow myself to be alone with her/him in a dark room."
- "If I kiss, it will always be when I'm standing."
- "I will bring coloring books on dates. When things heat up, we will begin coloring. (Unbelievable? It's true! This couple became one of the heads of Child Evangelism in Salem, Oregon.)

Some of these rules may seem ridiculous to you, so make up your own! _____
_____
_____
_____
_____
_____
_____
_____
_____
_____

A final thought on marriage and divorce: During World War II, Winston Churchill, the Prime Minister of England, said: *"Never give in. Never give in. Never, never, never, never—in nothing, great or small, large or petty—never give in, except to convictions of honour and good sense…"*13 In other words, **stand tall** when it comes to God's commands, never, never, never giving in to something that is not of Him, as with premarital sex and divorce. If this sounds like it is asking too much**, *take heart,*** for if you have accepted Jesus Christ as your Lord and Savior, you have the **HOLY SPIRIT** living within you to help you **stand Tall** in the toughest of circumstances: *"I **CAN** do all things **through Christ** who strengthens me!"* **[Philippians 4:13]**

Now is the time for you to draw the line,

STEP OVER IT,

move into your future, and never look back!

DIGGING IN – WEEK SEVEN – GROUP TIME

Jesus Stands Tall under Persecution

Just, sinless, pure, and perfect—Jesus was surrounded by crowds. Sometimes they listened well as He taught them how to live and pray: *"Do to others whatever you would like them to do to you. This is the essence of all that is taught in the law and the prophets."* **[Matt. 7:12]** *"Pray like this: Our Father in heaven, may your name be kept holy…"* **[Matt. 6: 9]** Once they shouted in adoration: *"Praise God! Blessings on the one who comes in the name of the Lord! Blessing on the coming Kingdom of our ancestor David! Praise God in highest heaven!"* laying palm branches before Him as he rode on a donkey into Jerusalem. **[Matt. 21:9, Matt.21:15, Mark 11:9, Mark 11:10, John 12:13]** Yet ultimately, many of that same crowd with mob mentality shouted, "Crucify Him!" **[Matt 27:22-23]**

Clearly, Jesus was loved; and clearly, He was hated. He was respected, adored, then condemned. He was called Holy One of God, Lord…then blasphemer, demon, and criminal. As with us, Jesus felt hunger and suffered temptation; and as with us, He did not desire to endure the torture and crucifixion that He knew (as God) lay in front of Him: *"My Father! If it is possible, let this cup of suffering be taken away from me. Jesus said, 'yet I want your will to be done, not mine.'"* **[Matthew 26:39]**

Through it all, Jesus **stood tall** as He faced persecution. You may think this was easier for Him than for you because Jesus was God. Yes, and no! Truly, Jesus was and is **God**, fully and completely.

"<u>The Son radiates God's own glory</u> and <u>expresses the very character of God</u>, and He sustains everything by the mighty power of His command. When He had cleansed us from our sins, He sat down in the place of honor at the right hand of the majestic God in heaven." **[Hebrews 1:3]** Other versions, the HCS, NASB, and ESV, use the terms *<u>exact expression / image / imprint of God</u>* describing Jesus. **Jesus is God**.

Yet **Jesus also was and is man**, fully and completely…a mystery indeed!

"God became a human being without ceasing to be God." *D. Stewart* **1**

Look up **Philippians 2:6-8** and read from several versions.

1. What words are used to describe what Jesus did in becoming man?

- *"… but emptied Himself, by taking the form of a servant, being born in the likeness of men."* **ESV NASB HCS**
- *"…He gave up his divine privileges; He took the humble position of a slave and was born as a human being.* **NLT**

To better understand this, read the following summary written by Don Stewart for the Blue Letter Bible: *"When Jesus came* to earth He laid aside or emptied Himself of something. There are many misconceptions as to what He set aside. It was not His Deity. Jesus could not empty Himself of His Deity - He could not stop being God. He was always God the Son. He could not exchange His Deity for His humanity. Neither did He set aside only some of His divine attributes and keep others. In addition, Jesus always knew He was God and possessed these divine attributes - He was not ignorant of who He was or what He could do. Moreover Jesus allowed the people to know that He had such powers. Neither did Jesus set aside the use of His relative attributes such as being all-powerful, all-knowing, and everywhere present. Those powers were always present with Him.

When Jesus became a human being He divested Himself of certain rights as God the Son. This can be seen in three ways. First, He restricted Himself to a human body with all its limitations. He gave up His position when He became a human being. Second, He veiled or hid His glory from the people. Finally, He exercised His relative attributes only by the will of God the Father - never on His own initiative."[2]

Let's continue the mystery: As God, Jesus could not sin; but as a human, Jesus could if He chose to disobey His Father's will. Therefore, He was tested, just like you and me: *"This High Priest of ours understands our weaknesses, for He faced all of the same testings we do, yet He did not sin."* NLT *"For we do not have a high priest who is unable to sympathize with our weaknesses, but One who in every respect has been tempted as we are, yet without sin."* ESV **[Hebrews 4:15]**

Jesus, *as the Word and as the Son*, knew who He was, and as the Son of the Father, always turned to Him in prayer for direction and strength so He could act in accordance to His Father's will:

"When you have lifted up the Son of Man on the cross, then you will understand that I AM He. I do nothing on my own but say only what the Father taught me." **[John 8:28]**

This is how Jesus **stood tall**, withstanding the persecution of Satan, the Pharisees, other religious leaders, mockers, those who humiliated Him, betrayers, deniers, and murderers--all without sinning. He trusted His Father, prayed to Him, then lived in obedience to His Father's will, displaying dependence not on Himself, but on God the Father. What a great teacher for us to follow!

So, although Jesus could have reveled in displaying all His mighty powers, putting Marvel characters to shame, He exemplified humility, only revealing His divine nature when it was the will of God.

2. Describe in your words what this means. While Jesus, the Father, and the Holy Spirit were always one, Jesus purposely chose to be dependent upon His Father's will for direction after He became man, then acted upon that will and His Father's timing.

3. What power does Jesus display in **John 1:45-48**? Omniscience—knowing all things. Jesus makes it clear that He knows all things when He identifies Nathanael as a man of integrity and tells Nathanael He saw him sitting under a tree before Philip found him.

4. Read **Matthew 24:32-36**. Regarding the timing of Jesus' second return, what power does Jesus choose not to use, and why do you think He did this? He does not use His omniscience. Jesus chose not to be aware of the time of His second coming because that was His Father's will. Perhaps His Father willed this because He wanted mankind *always* to remain faithful to Him, trusting in God's perfect timing for that revelation.

Because Jesus chose to follow God's will, He faced horrific persecution. As we have already studied, He was attacked by Jewish religious leaders who falsely accused Him of defying God's commands when He performed miracles on the Sabbath, all because of His love and compassion for people. When He taught the truth, those same religious leaders would try to trap Him through *trick* questions. For a time, even His own family misunderstood who He was. Then came the worst persecution of all: the trial before Pilate, the shouts for crucifixion, the mocking of the soldiers, and finally, whipping and crucifixion.

Try for a moment to picture yourself being stripped of your clothing, having a robe imitating royalty placed on you, a crown of thorns jammed on your head, being handed a fake scepter made of reeds, then having troops kneel before you in false adulation, spitting upon you and striking you on your head now crowned with those thorns. Imagine being whipped mercilessly; while bleeding out, you are forced to carry a cross to Golgatha and then have nails driven through your hands and feet. All the while you are derided by the mocking of the of the Roman soldiers and the two criminals crucified next to you (what a praise that one of them recognizes who you are and asks for salvation!).

Now, you and I **DO** deserve this fate because of our sins, but Jesus did not. At this point, did He desire a different destiny? Read some of His words: *"My soul is crushed with grief to the point of death."* **[Matthew 26:38a]** *"My Father! If it is possible, let this cup of suffering be taken away from Me. Yet I want Your will to be done, not Mine."* **[Matthew 26:39]**

Before acting, then, Jesus sought God's will and lived in obedience to that. He could have rebelled and called upon His Father's angelic host of warriors to change His fate, but He did not. Again, Jesus ***always*** acted within the Father's will and timing.

Why was all this necessary? In Genesis chapters one and two, God created a perfect world, but in Genesis chapter 3 came ***the fall***: Adam, the first man, rebelled against God by falling into sin's temptation, bringing death into the world; at this point every man was doomed to die, being separated from God forever. But our awesome, loving, and compassionate God is *jealous* for us, desiring no one to perish: *"He does not want anyone to be destroyed, but wants everyone to repent."* **[2 Peter 3:9b]**

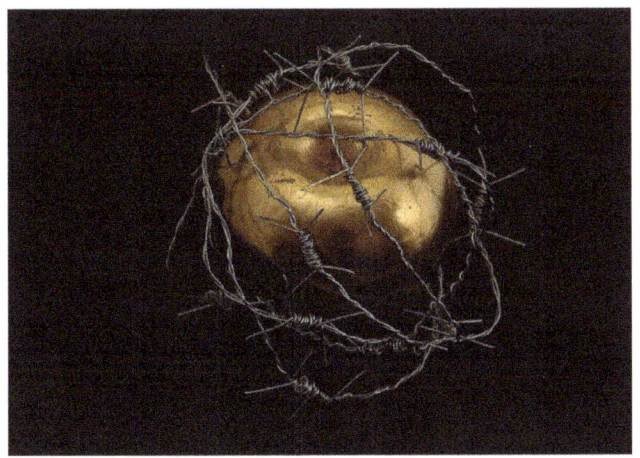

Jesus died to conquer sin and it's temptations.

God now needed a perfect, sinless man to become a second Adam, one who would resist temptation, take all mankind's sins upon Himself, and through a sacrificial death, provide a path to eternal life. But there is no man throughout the ages who has not sinned: *"For everyone has sinned; we all fall short of God's glorious standard."* **[Romans 3:23]** So God made a selfless choice—that of sending His only Son, Jesus, to be that perfect man; and Jesus, as "the Word," made the selfless choice to step out of His kingdom and become a baby, knowing He would have to grow as a man, resist temptation, and take man's sins upon Himself as He would become man's sacrificial lamb through crucifixion.

Read **Romans 5:12** and **1 Cor. 15:22**. Sum up what these verses say. As Adam did not follow God's will when he ate of the tree of knowledge of good and evil, disobeying God and allowing sin to enter the world (**Romans 5:12**), Jesus' task, as *the second Adam*, was to perfectly obey His Father's will, removing sin when people accepted Him as their Savior. (**1 Cor. 15:22**)

Persecution—being falsely accused, betrayed, harassed and attacked verbally and/or physically—is something no one looks forward to. Reality is, however, all of us will face this in some manner during our lives, and even as I type, Christians in many countries are enduring extreme persecution, being chased from homes, imprisoned, tortured, or killed for Christ. *"Do you remember what I told you? 'A slave is not greater than the master.' Since they persecuted Me, naturally they will persecute you. And if they had listened to Me, they would listen to you."* **[John 15:20]** *"God blesses you when people mock you and persecute you and lie about you and say all sorts of evil things against you because you are My followers."* **[Matthew 5:11]** *"If the world hates you, remember that it hated Me first."* **[John 15:18]** *"Dear friends, don't be surprised at the fiery trials you are going through, as if something strange were happening to you."* **[1 Peter 4:12]**

For you, persecution may mean losing certain sets of friends, being mocked, jilted, ridiculed, or possibly slandered by others. Then there's always the potential of Christ coming back in your lifetime!

Teen persecution *Christ's return will be seen by ALL!*

Depending upon that timing--pre-tribulation, mid-tribulation, pre-wrath, post-tribulation--you may be faced with physical persecution. (Briefly discuss these.)

How are you to face this? *"Instead, be very glad—for these trials make you partners with Christ in His suffering, so that you will have the wonderful joy of seeing His glory when it is revealed to all the world."* **[1 Peter 4: 13]**

When facing persecution, we are to **stand tall**, understanding the great rewards we will receive in heaven as believers who stand firmly in Christ. We are not to live in fear, but in the joyous expectation of living forever in the love and grace of the triune God—the beauty and peace of which we cannot possibly imagine.

Personal Time – Week Seven – Day One

Define persecution and explain what you have learned.

Personal Time – Week Seven – Day Two

Have you ever suffered from persecution? Was this because you are a believer in Christ or not? If you have been persecuted, was it physical or verbal (harassing, etc.)? What was your response, and was it what it should have been?

OR

Have you ever persecuted another for his/her faith or otherwise? If so, what action(s) should you now take? Suggestions: Accept Christ as Savior, if not done so previously; ask God for forgiveness; ask the person persecuted for forgiveness; make retribution if needed and possible.

OR

If you've never suffered from persecution, write a note to God. Consider thanking Him for giving you a life free from persecution so far, but asking Him for His direction and strength when you will face life's trials in the future. _____

_____
_____
_____
_____
_____
_____
_____
_____

Personal Time – Week Seven – Day Three

Jesus accepted and suffered extreme persecution for our sakes. What do you think were some of the rewards for Him in doing so? Ideas: His obedience pleased the Father; He had the joy of bringing all believers into a permanent, immortal, loving relationship with the Father, Himself, and the Holy Spirit.

Personal Time – Week Seven – Day Four

God the Father and Jesus **stood tall**, making selfless choices. Say a prayer while carefully examining your life. Would you consider yourself a self-centered or selfless person? Give examples. If self-centered, would you like to change? Give some examples of some selfless acts you believe would bless others. Now pray to the Father and ask for strength to **stand tall** and follow-through. Part of your prayer may be, *"For I can do everything through Christ, who gives me strength."* **[Philippians 4:13]** _____

_____
_____
_____
_____
_____
_____
_____
_____
_____

DIGGING IN – WEEK EIGHT – GROUP TIME

Personal Reflection

This study has taken us on quite a journey, from what it means to **stand tall** to understanding hypocrisy, blind leaders, marriage, divorce, and persecution. Much of this has involved head knowledge, but if what you have learned stops there, then the mission of this study is incomplete. To have a relationship with Christ, your head knowledge must move into your heart. It is only when you have hearts changed by Christ, you can **stand tall** against our culture's hypocrisy, ungodly leaders, challenges to God's design for men, women, their roles in marriage, and persecution.

During this final time together, I would ask you to read the following verses on **standing tall**, then take time to pray about each of them. Ask yourself if any of these verses have applied to you in the past, do so now, or will in the future. How will you react to their truths? How will you **stand tall**?

If you wish, you may write down what God places on your heart as you read each section, or you may choose to wait until you have finished praying over all the verses to write what God places on your heart. ***This is a personal time for you and the Lord,*** and it is up to you whether or not you choose to write down your thoughts. Leaders, use this as a quiet time for teens to read verses, reflect on them, then write their answers. As this is a personal time, there is no need to discuss answers unless you and the teens wish to do so.

My Heart Check

Do I/Will I Stand Tall with Boldness?

- **Ephesians 6:10-14** *"A final word: Be strong in the Lord and in His mighty power. Put on all of God's armor so that you will be able to stand firm against all strategies of the devil. For we are not fighting against flesh-and-blood enemies, but against evil rulers and authorities of the unseen world, against mighty powers in this dark world, and against evil spirits in the heavenly places. Therefore, put on every piece of God's armor so you will be able to resist the enemy in the time of evil. Then after the battle you will still be standing firm. Stand your ground, putting on the belt of truth and the body armor of God's righteousness."*

- **Corinthians 1:21-22** *"It is God who enables us, along with you, to stand firm for Christ. He has commissioned us, and He has identified us as His own by placing the Holy Spirit in our hearts as the first installment that guarantees everything He has promised us."*

- **Philippians 4:13** *"For I can do everything through Christ, who gives me strength."* _____

_____

_____

_____

_____

_____

Do I/Will I StandTall under Persecution?

- **Matthew 10:22** *"You will be hated by everyone because of Me, but the one who stands firm to the end will be saved."*
- **1 Peter 5:9** *"Resist him (Satan) and be firm in the faith, because you know that your brothers throughout the world are undergoing the same kinds of suffering."*

Do I/Will I Stand Tall Practicing Endurance?

- **1 Corinthians 15:58** *"So, my dear brothers and sisters, be strong and immovable. Always work enthusiastically for the Lord, for you know that nothing you do for the Lord is ever useless."*
- **Matthew 24:13** *"But the one who endures to the end will be saved."*
- **James 1:12** *"A man who endures trials is blessed, because when he passes the test he will receive the crown of life that God has promised to those who love Him."*

Do I/Will I Stand Tall in God's Truths?

- **Galatians 5:1** *"So Christ has truly set us free. Now make sure that you stay free, and don't get tied up again in slavery to the law."*

- **1 Timothy 6:12** *"Fight the good fight for the true faith. Hold tightly to the eternal life to which God has called you, which you have declared so well before many witnesses."*

My final heart check:

Do I understand how much God loves me and what Jesus did for me? "**John 3:16** *"For this is how God loved the world: He gave His one and only Son, so that everyone who believes in Him will not perish but have eternal life."*

Do I fully understand that there is only one path to heaven? **John 14:6** *"Jesus told him, "I am the way, the truth, and the life. No one can come to the Father except through Me."*

Do I love Jesus with all my heart, mind, soul, and strength? *Is He my treasure and my number one in life*—the Lord over all I am now and will become? *Is He my Savior?* Does **Psalm 34**, penned by Moses, resound in my heart?

> *Shout with joy to the LORD, all the earth!*
> *Worship the LORD with gladness.*
> *Come before Him, singing with joy.*
> *Acknowledge that the LORD is God!*
> *He made us, and we are His.*
> *We are his people, the sheep of His pasture.*
> *Enter His gates with thanksgiving;*
> *go into His courts with praise.*
> *Give thanks to Him and praise His name.*
> *For the LORD is good.*
> *His unfailing love continues forever,*
> *and His faithfulness continues to each generation.*

Can I read the following poem and know it is true for me?

DEEP in the heart of me,

Nothing but You!

See through the art of me—

Deep in the heart of me

Find the best part of me,

Changeless and true.

Deep in the heart of me,

Nothing but YOU!

Ruth Guthrie Harding [3]

_____

_____

_____

_____

After examining these things, ask yourself, "Can I say with conviction that I have this kind of heart because of my love for Jesus? In fact, can I say with conviction that I have **with all my heart accepted Jesus Christ as my Lord and Savior**?"

If you have any doubt, there is no better time than now to shout out **"Jesus I need you!"** Following is a prayer you may say to ask Jesus to become your Savior.

MY PRAYER FOR SALVATION

Jesus, I have carefully considered my life, who I am without You, and who I will become with You. To change, I recognize that I desperately need You in my life, and today _____ (today's date), I, _____ (your name), am asking You to adopt me into Your family.

I know and confess that I am a sinner and recognize there is nothing I can do to rescue myself from my sins. I ask for Your forgiveness, knowing that You, pure and sinless, already willingly took those sins upon Yourself, died in my place, then rose in victory from the dead. You did all this so I can live with You forever.

So from this moment on, Jesus, I commit my life to You, asking You to rule over me as my Lord and Savior. Thank you for accepting me for who I am, but know that I am relying on Your promise to fill me with Your Holy Spirit so that I might live as a new creation, dedicated and obedient to you. Jesus, I will praise your name forever!

CONGRATULATIONS! If you prayed this prayer, or one of your own asking Jesus to be your Savior, you are now a child of God and a full inheritor of all His promises! You can look forward to spending an eternity of joy and peace with the One who loves you above all measure, delighting in and glorifying Him.

*NOW CHOOSE TO
STAND TALL . . .
FIRM IN YOUR FAITH
AND IN THE ONE
WHO GAVE HIS ALL!*

We've now spent quite some time together, time in which you've been challenged to study biblical truths and to carefully examine your heart. Based on this, space is provided for you below for you to write down any of your thoughts. Perhaps you have new convictions and corresponding *unshakable unbreakables*, or perhaps you'd like to write a prayer or poem to our awesome God. Whatever He is placing on your heart, write that down. He's right here with you, He loves you, cares for you, and He's listening! _____

You _____ (write your name) are special! You are valued and loved more than you could ever imagine by our Almighty God who showed us by example what love really is! May He—our all-compassionate, merciful, and loving Father—bless you every day, and may you lock this blessing and following prayer I wish for you deep within your hearts:

*"May the LORD bless you and protect you. May the L*ORD *smile on you and be gracious to you. May the L*ORD *show you His favor and give you His peace."* **[Numbers 6:24-26]**

"I pray that from His glorious, unlimited resources He will empower you with inner strength through His Spirit. Then Christ will make His home in your hearts as you trust in Him. Your roots will grow down into God's love and keep you strong. And may you have the power to understand, as all God's people should, how wide, how long, how high, and how deep His love is. May you experience the love of Christ, though it is too great to understand fully. Then you will be made complete with all the fullness of life and power that comes from God." **[Eph 3: 16-19]**

Candice Mary Thomas

ACKNOWLEDGEMENTS

This work is what God put on my heart to accomplish, and though it has taken close to several years to write, I pray that it will honor Him by impacting your lives, helping you walk in Jesus' way, becoming more like Him each day.

To my husband, Terry, I give thanks for well…everything! He has encouraged me in my writing, patiently endured "my mess" as I scattered books and papers over our dining room table day after day, and worked endless hours while taking valuable time away from him. Without his support, this study would not have been possible. (And without his leading, I would not have found the Lord!)

I also wish to thank the pastors who have impacted and enriched my life for over forty years now, especially Vaughn Nelson, Dale James, Jerry Franz, and Ray Birch. These pastors either introduced me to Christ or spent hours helping me grow in Him as we worked together in our Lord's service and as friends. Thanks also to the pastors of Edgewater Christian Fellowship (Matt Heverly, Mark Skudstad, and Dick Worthington) who took time to discuss with me the topics of marriage and divorce and who faithfully teach God's Word to reach the unsaved.

To Dale James I owe special thanks for reviewing my chapters on marriage and divorce and to Ray Birch, for reviewing my entire study for theological soundness along with his in-debth comments, explanations, and suggestions for improvement. I would be more than horrified to lead any child (or adult) astray from God's Word, and Ray has helped me to be accurate biblically and to add more depth to needed areas.

Thanks, also, to my wonderful friend and editor, Sandy Birch, whose bright eyes catch things mine don't! You are awesome! I pray our Lord will bless you more abundantly than you ever could imagine!

P.S. If there are any "glitches" in this work such as misspellings, punctuation, etc., I claim all responsibility!

NOTES/SOURCES

Week One
1. https://en.wiktionary.org/wiki/stand_tall
2. https://ebible.com/questions/7384-how-old-were-daniel-shadrach-meshach-and-abednego-when-they-were-youths-in-Babylon
https://www.quora.com/How-old-was-Daniel-in-the-Bible-when-he-was-taken-captive
3. https://www.heartbeatinternational.org/whats-in-a-name
4. https://www.britannica.com/topic/Marduk
5. https://www.heartbeatinternational.org/whats-in-a-name
6. https://www.behindthename.com/name/shadrach
7. https://www.heartbeatinternational.org/whats-in-a-name
8. https://www.heartbeatinternational.org/whats-in-a-name
9. https://www.behindthename.com/name/abednego

Week Two
1. https://bibleproject.com/learn/the-law/
https://www.merriam-webster.com/dictionary/Pentateuch
2. https://www.jewfaq.org/613.htm
3. Did God Also Give Moses an Oral Law? Dr. Eitan Bar. May 30, 2016. https://www.oneforisrael.org/bible-based-teaching-from-israel/did-god-also-give-oses-an-oral-law/
4. What is the Oral Torah? Naftali Silberberg. https:www.chabad.org/library/article_cdo/aid/812102/jewish/What-is-the-Oral-Torah.htm
5. Fifth Commandment: Honor Your other and Father. Mike Bennett. https://lifehopeandtruth.com/bible/10-commandments/honor-fifth-commandment/
6. Confusing Man's Traditions with God's Commandments: Part 2. John MacArthur. https://www.gty.org/library/sermons-library/2312/confusing-mans-traditions-with-gods-commandments-part-2

7. Torah Sheba'al Peh-The Oral Torah and Jewish Tradition. John J. Parsons. https://hebrew4christians.com/Articles/Oral Torah/oral_torah.html.
8. Shabbat: What is Shabbat? https://www.jewishvirtuallibrary.org/what-is-shabbat-jewish-Sabbath
9. What Did Jesus Say about the Sabbath? Administrator. March 10, 2015. https://messianicsabbath.com/2015/03/10/what-did-jesus-say-about-the-sabbath/
10. Spring Sports and Sunday Church—Five Suggestions for Parents. Tony Reinke. April 17, 2018. https://www.desiringgod.org/articles/spring-sports-and-Sunday-church
11. Sports on Sundays: the Consequences of Skipping Church. Steve Turley. July 21, 2017. https://www.turleytalks.com/blog-summary/sports-on-Sundays-the-consequences-of-skipping-Church

Week Three
1. https://www.phrases.org.uk/meanings/67150.html
2. https://www.wycliffe.net/resources/statistics/
3. https://www.focusonthefamily.com/family-qa/blasphemy-of-the-holy-spirit-and-the-unforgivable-sin/

Week Four
1. https://www.gotquestions.org/breath-of-life.html
2. These are typical Protestant wedding vows, but in looking at the various religions, all involve pledging or vowing a lifelong relationship. https://www.theknot.com/content/traditional-wedding-vows-from-various-religions
3. Sonnet 116. William Shakespeare. https://www.goodreads.com/quotes/95300-love-is-not-love-which-alters-when-it-alteration-finds
4. Quote. Dietrich Bonhoeffer. https://www.goodreads.com/quotes/576863-as-you-gave-the-ring-to-one-another-and-have

WeekFive: I was directed to a fantastic sermon on marriage by David Whiting from New Heights Church in Vancouver, Washington, a few weeks ago. I would recommend adding an extra week to watch this sermon at the conclusion of Week Five. Look for May 30, 2021-- "God's Perfect Design for Marriage." https://newheights.org

Week Six
1. The Road Not Taken. Robert Frost. August, 1915. https://www.poetryfoundation.org/poems/44272/the-road-not-taken
2. Regular Church Attenders Marry More and Divorce Less Than Their Less Devout Peers. Brian Hollar. March 4, 2020. https://ifstudies.org/blog/regular-church-attenders-marry-more-and-divorce-less-than-their-less-devout-peers
3. HCSB Large Print Study Bible, 2015, Holman Bible Publishers, Nashville, Tennessee, p. 1593, footnote 2:16
4. Jesus on Divorce PDF. Dave Brisban. April 20, 2005. theeffect.org.>wp>-content>uploads>2016>Jesus-on-divorce
5. https://www.jewishvirtuallibrary.org/hillel-and-shammai
6. https://crossref-it.info/articles/618/rabbi-pharisee-teacher-of-the-law
7. What Did Jesus Say about Divorce? Chuck Swindoll. May 07, 2013 https://www.insight.org/resources/article-library/individual/what-did-jesus-say-about-divorce
8. Quotable Quotes. Matthew Henry. https://www.goodreads.com/quotes/104025-eve-was-not-taken-out-of-adam-s-head-to-top
9. Larry King's magnificent seven—his ex-wives. Dana Kennedy. January 23, 2021. https://nypost.com/2021/01/23/larry-kings-magnificent-seven-his-ex-wives/
10. What Reasons Does the Bible Give for Divorce? Mark Driscoll. https://realfaith.com/daily-deotions/what-reasons-does-the-

bible-give-for-divorce
11. What are the Effects of Divorce on Children? https://www.familymeans.org/effects-of-divorce-on-children.html
12. When, and Why, Divorce Hurts Kids. https://ifstudies.org/blog/when-and-why-divorce-hurts-kids
13. Mere Christianity, Book 3, Chapter 6, "Christian Marriage." https://www.goodreads.com/quotes/139097-the-christian-idea-of-marriage-is-based-on-christ-s-words
14. Never Give In, Never, Never Never. Winston Churchill. October 29, 1941. https://www.nationalchurchillmuseum.org/never-give-in-never-never-never.html

Week Seven

1. In What Sense Did Jesus Empty Himself? (Kenosis, Condescension of Christ). Don Stewart. https://www.blueletterbible.org/fac/don_stewart/don_stewart_795.cfm
2. In What Sense Did Jesus Empty Himself? (Kenosis, Condescension of Christ). Don Stewart. https://www.blueletterbible.org/fac/don_stewart/don_stewart_795.cfm
3. You. Ruth Guthrie Hardig. Jesse B. Rittenhouse, ed. (1869-1948). *The Second Book of Modern Verse*. 1922. https://www.bartleby.com/271/60.html

APPENDIX A

PRAYER FOR SALVATION

    Jesus, I have carefully considered my life, who I am without You, and who I will become with You. To change, I recognize that I desperately need You in my life, and today _____ (today's date), I, _____ (your name), am asking You to adopt me into Your family.

    I know and confess that I am a sinner and recognize there is nothing I can do to rescue myself from my sins. I ask for Your forgiveness, knowing that You, pure and sinless, already willingly took those sins upon Yourself, died in my place, then rose in victory from the dead. You did all this so I can live with You forever.

    So from this moment on, Jesus, I commit my life to You, asking You to rule over me as my Lord and Savior. Thank you for accepting me for who I am, but know that I am relying on Your promise to fill me with Your Holy Spirit so that I might live as a new creation, dedicated and obedient to you. Jesus, I will praise your name forever!

Glossary

Christ: Derived from the Greek word *Christos* meaning "the anointed or chosen one"

Complement (verb): to complete, make better or more perfect

Covenant: An unbreakable promise

Eunuch: A male who is castrated (made sterile by having his testicles removed) to prevent sexual drive or having children.

Jesus: Savior

Legalism: Strict adherence to a system of rules or laws to obtain salvation rather than understanding we are saved by grace, and being saved, we are to have hearts set on loving God and loving people.

Messiah: Derived from the Hebrew word *Mashiach*, meaning "the anointed or chosen one"

Pharisees: There were three major sects of Jews in Jesus' time—the Pharisees, the Essenes, and the Sadducees. The Pharisees' name came from the Aramaic word, *peras* meaning *to separate*, and they purposely lived differently from the general Jewish public trying to display adherence to all Jewish oral and written laws, both of which they believed in. Their righteousness became external as they became more interested in outward appearance than inward spiritual growth. Pharisees believed in the resurrection of the dead, the immortality of the soul, and rewards based upon works.

Sadducees: These men believed **only** in Jewish written law. They denied the resurrection of the body, the immortality of the soul, and any spiritual world. They discredited John the Baptist and joined with the Pharisees in opposing Jesus, desiring Him to be put to death.

Sanhedrin: This was the highest Jewish court consisting of seventy members drawn from chief priests, scribes, and elders, who made final decisions regarding Mosaic Law until 70 AD, when the second temple was destroyed. This court could order arrests but could not sentence anyone to death. The president was called the *high priest*.

Scribes Today we would call them lawyers. They were scholars who preserved, transcribed, developed and taught the Jewish laws used in courts. Originally Levites and priests, scribes later became mostly laymen. They held no political power, but were highly regarded by the Jews, becoming their leaders. They desired admiration from their pupils and the general public, becoming more concerned with the outer appearance of holiness than with actually helping Jews grow in righteousness. Luke wrote, *"What sorrow awaits you experts in religious law! For you remove the key to knowledge from the people. You don't enter the Kingdom yourselves, and you prevent others from entering."* They became fierce opponents of Jesus and played a major part in His being arrested and crucified.

Unshakable Unbreakable: Based on convictions, unshakable unbreakables are commitments you make now that will help you follow God's will when you face tough choices and decisions in life.

BIBLIOGRAPHY

Barber, and Merrill F. Unger. *The New Unger's Bible Dictionary*. Chicago: Moody Press, 1988.

"complement" Merriam-Webster.com. Merriam-Webster, 1858. Web. 7 May 2021.

English Standard Version. Bible Gateway. Web. 2019-2020.

Holman Christian Standard Version. Web. 2019-2020.

Holman Christian Standard Large Print Study Bible. 2015. Nashville: Holman Bible Publishers

New American Standard Bible. Bible Gateway. Web. 2019-2020.

New King James Cultural Backgrounds Study Bible. 2017. Grand Rapids, MI: Zondervan, 2002.

New Living Translation. Web. 2019-2020.

Tenney, Merrill C. and Cruden, Alexander. The Handy Bible Dictionary and Concordance. Grand Rapids, MI:Zondervan, 1983.

Vine, W E, Merrill F. Unger, William White, and W E. Vine. *Vine's Complete Expository Dictionary of Old and New Testament Words*. Nashville: Nelson, 1985. Print.

NOTES

NOTES

www.ingramcontent.com/pod-product-compliance
Lightning Source LLC
Chambersburg PA
CBHW061727070526
44583CB00024B/3035